Mometrix
TEST PREPARATION

I0889386

CLEP®

US History II Exam Secrets Study Guide

Dear Future Exam Success Story

First of all, **THANK YOU** for purchasing Mometrix study materials!

Second, congratulations! You are one of the few determined test-takers who are committed to doing whatever it takes to excel on your exam. **You have come to the right place.** We developed these study materials with one goal in mind: to deliver you the information you need in a format that's concise and easy to use.

In addition to optimizing your guide for the content of the test, we've outlined our recommended steps for breaking down the preparation process into small, attainable goals so you can make sure you stay on track.

We've also analyzed the entire test-taking process, identifying the most common pitfalls and showing how you can overcome them and be ready for any curveball the test throws you.

Standardized testing is one of the biggest obstacles on your road to success, which only increases the importance of doing well in the high-pressure, high-stakes environment of test day. Your results on this test could have a significant impact on your future, and this guide provides the information and practical advice to help you achieve your full potential on test day.

Your success is our success

We would love to hear from you! If you would like to share the story of your exam success or if you have any questions or comments in regard to our products, please contact us at **800-673-8175** or **support@mometrix.com**.

Thanks again for your business and we wish you continued success!

Sincerely,
The Mometrix Test Preparation Team

Need more help? Check out our flashcards at:
http://MometrixFlashcards.com/CLEP

TABLE OF CONTENTS

Introduction

Thank you for purchasing this resource! You have made the choice to prepare yourself for a test that could have a huge impact on your future, and this guide is designed to help you be fully ready for test day. Obviously, it's important to have a solid understanding of the test material, but you also need to be prepared for the unique environment and stressors of the test, so that you can perform to the best of your abilities.

For this purpose, the first section that appears in this guide is the **Secret Keys**. We've devoted countless hours to meticulously researching what works and what doesn't, and we've boiled down our findings to the five most impactful steps you can take to improve your performance on the test. We start at the beginning with study planning and move through the preparation process, all the way to the testing strategies that will help you get the most out of what you know when you're finally sitting in front of the test.

We recommend that you start preparing for your test as far in advance as possible. However, if you've bought this guide as a last-minute study resource and only have a few days before your test, we recommend that you skip over the first two Secret Keys since they address a long-term study plan.

If you struggle with **test anxiety**, we strongly encourage you to check out our recommendations for how you can overcome it. Test anxiety is a formidable foe, but it can be beaten, and we want to make sure you have the tools you need to defeat it.

Secret Key #1 – Plan Big, Study Small

There's a lot riding on your performance. If you want to ace this test, you're going to need to keep your skills sharp and the material fresh in your mind. You need a plan that lets you review everything you need to know while still fitting in your schedule. We'll break this strategy down into three categories.

Information Organization

Start with the information you already have: the official test outline. From this, you can make a complete list of all the concepts you need to cover before the test. Organize these concepts into groups that can be studied together, and create a list of any related vocabulary you need to learn so you can brush up on any difficult terms. You'll want to keep this vocabulary list handy once you actually start studying since you may need to add to it along the way.

Time Management

Once you have your set of study concepts, decide how to spread them out over the time you have left before the test. Break your study plan into small, clear goals so you have a manageable task for each day and know exactly what you're doing. Then just focus on one small step at a time. When you manage your time this way, you don't need to spend hours at a time studying. Studying a small block of content for a short period each day helps you retain information better and avoid stressing over how much you have left to do. You can relax knowing that you have a plan to cover everything in time. In order for this strategy to be effective though, you have to start studying early and stick to your schedule. Avoid the exhaustion and futility that comes from last-minute cramming!

Study Environment

The environment you study in has a big impact on your learning. Studying in a coffee shop, while probably more enjoyable, is not likely to be as fruitful as studying in a quiet room. It's important to keep distractions to a minimum. You're only planning to study for a short block of time, so make the most of it. Don't pause to check your phone or get up to find a snack. It's also important to **avoid multitasking**. Research has consistently shown that multitasking will make your studying dramatically less effective. Your study area should also be comfortable and well-lit so you don't have the distraction of straining your eyes or sitting on an uncomfortable chair.

The time of day you study is also important. You want to be rested and alert. Don't wait until just before bedtime. Study when you'll be most likely to comprehend and remember. Even better, if you know what time of day your test will be, set that time aside for study. That way your brain will be used to working on that subject at that specific time and you'll have a better chance of recalling information.

Finally, it can be helpful to team up with others who are studying for the same test. Your actual studying should be done in as isolated an environment as possible, but the work of organizing the information and setting up the study plan can be divided up. In between study sessions, you can discuss with your teammates the concepts that you're all studying and quiz each other on the details. Just be sure that your teammates are as serious about the test as you are. If you find that your study time is being replaced with social time, you might need to find a new team.

Secret Key #2 – Make Your Studying Count

You're devoting a lot of time and effort to preparing for this test, so you want to be absolutely certain it will pay off. This means doing more than just reading the content and hoping you can remember it on test day. It's important to make every minute of study count. There are two main areas you can focus on to make your studying count.

Retention

It doesn't matter how much time you study if you can't remember the material. You need to make sure you are retaining the concepts. To check your retention of the information you're learning, try recalling it at later times with minimal prompting. Try carrying around flashcards and glance at one or two from time to time or ask a friend who's also studying for the test to quiz you.

To enhance your retention, look for ways to put the information into practice so that you can apply it rather than simply recalling it. If you're using the information in practical ways, it will be much easier to remember. Similarly, it helps to solidify a concept in your mind if you're not only reading it to yourself but also explaining it to someone else. Ask a friend to let you teach them about a concept you're a little shaky on (or speak aloud to an imaginary audience if necessary). As you try to summarize, define, give examples, and answer your friend's questions, you'll understand the concepts better and they will stay with you longer. Finally, step back for a big picture view and ask yourself how each piece of information fits with the whole subject. When you link the different concepts together and see them working together as a whole, it's easier to remember the individual components.

Finally, practice showing your work on any multi-step problems, even if you're just studying. Writing out each step you take to solve a problem will help solidify the process in your mind, and you'll be more likely to remember it during the test.

Modality

Modality simply refers to the means or method by which you study. Choosing a study modality that fits your own individual learning style is crucial. No two people learn best in exactly the same way, so it's important to know your strengths and use them to your advantage.

For example, if you learn best by visualization, focus on visualizing a concept in your mind and draw an image or a diagram. Try color-coding your notes, illustrating them, or creating symbols that will trigger your mind to recall a learned concept. If you learn best by hearing or discussing information, find a study partner who learns the same way or read aloud to yourself. Think about how to put the information in your own words. Imagine that you are giving a lecture on the topic and record yourself so you can listen to it later.

For any learning style, flashcards can be helpful. Organize the information so you can take advantage of spare moments to review. Underline key words or phrases. Use different colors for different categories. Mnemonic devices (such as creating a short list in which every item starts with the same letter) can also help with retention. Find what works best for you and use it to store the information in your mind most effectively and easily.

Secret Key #3 – Practice the Right Way

Your success on test day depends not only on how many hours you put into preparing, but also on whether you prepared the right way. It's good to check along the way to see if your studying is paying off. One of the most effective ways to do this is by taking practice tests to evaluate your progress. Practice tests are useful because they show exactly where you need to improve. Every time you take a practice test, pay special attention to these three groups of questions:

- The questions you got wrong
- The questions you had to guess on, even if you guessed right
- The questions you found difficult or slow to work through

This will show you exactly what your weak areas are, and where you need to devote more study time. Ask yourself why each of these questions gave you trouble. Was it because you didn't understand the material? Was it because you didn't remember the vocabulary? Do you need more repetitions on this type of question to build speed and confidence? Dig into those questions and figure out how you can strengthen your weak areas as you go back to review the material.

Additionally, many practice tests have a section explaining the answer choices. It can be tempting to read the explanation and think that you now have a good understanding of the concept. However, an explanation likely only covers part of the question's broader context. Even if the explanation makes perfect sense, **go back and investigate** every concept related to the question until you're positive you have a thorough understanding.

As you go along, keep in mind that the practice test is just that: practice. Memorizing these questions and answers will not be very helpful on the actual test because it is unlikely to have any of the same exact questions. If you only know the right answers to the sample questions, you won't be prepared for the real thing. **Study the concepts** until you understand them fully, and then you'll be able to answer any question that shows up on the test.

It's important to wait on the practice tests until you're ready. If you take a test on your first day of study, you may be overwhelmed by the amount of material covered and how much you need to learn. Work up to it gradually.

On test day, you'll need to be prepared for answering questions, managing your time, and using the test-taking strategies you've learned. It's a lot to balance, like a mental marathon that will have a big impact on your future. Like training for a marathon, you'll need to start slowly and work your way up. When test day arrives, you'll be ready.

Start with the strategies you've read in the first two Secret Keys—plan your course and study in the way that works best for you. If you have time, consider using multiple study resources to get different approaches to the same concepts. It can be helpful to see difficult concepts from more than one angle. Then find a good source for practice tests. Many times, the test website will suggest potential study resources or provide sample tests.

Practice Test Strategy

If you're able to find at least three practice tests, we recommend this strategy:

Untimed and Open-Book Practice

Take the first test with no time constraints and with your notes and study guide handy. Take your time and focus on applying the strategies you've learned.

Timed and Open-Book Practice

Take the second practice test open-book as well, but set a timer and practice pacing yourself to finish in time.

Timed and Closed-Book Practice

Take any other practice tests as if it were test day. Set a timer and put away your study materials. Sit at a table or desk in a quiet room, imagine yourself at the testing center, and answer questions as quickly and accurately as possible.

Keep repeating timed and closed-book tests on a regular basis until you run out of practice tests or it's time for the actual test. Your mind will be ready for the schedule and stress of test day, and you'll be able to focus on recalling the material you've learned.

Secret Key #4 – Pace Yourself

Once you're fully prepared for the material on the test, your biggest challenge on test day will be managing your time. Just knowing that the clock is ticking can make you panic even if you have plenty of time left. Work on pacing yourself so you can build confidence against the time constraints of the exam. Pacing is a difficult skill to master, especially in a high-pressure environment, so **practice is vital**.

Set time expectations for your pace based on how much time is available. For example, if a section has 60 questions and the time limit is 30 minutes, you know you have to average 30 seconds or less per question in order to answer them all. Although 30 seconds is the hard limit, set 25 seconds per question as your goal, so you reserve extra time to spend on harder questions. When you budget extra time for the harder questions, you no longer have any reason to stress when those questions take longer to answer.

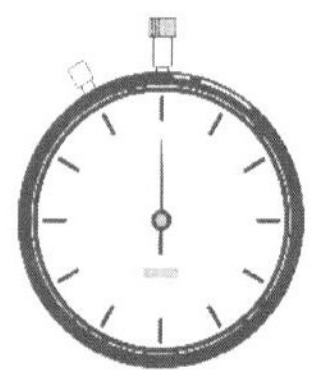

Don't let this time expectation distract you from working through the test at a calm, steady pace, but keep it in mind so you don't spend too much time on any one question. Recognize that taking extra time on one question you don't understand may keep you from answering two that you do understand later in the test. If your time limit for a question is up and you're still not sure of the answer, mark it and move on, and come back to it later if the time and the test format allow. If the testing format doesn't allow you to return to earlier questions, just make an educated guess; then put it out of your mind and move on.

On the easier questions, be careful not to rush. It may seem wise to hurry through them so you have more time for the challenging ones, but it's not worth missing one if you know the concept and just didn't take the time to read the question fully. Work efficiently but make sure you understand the question and have looked at all of the answer choices, since more than one may seem right at first.

Even if you're paying attention to the time, you may find yourself a little behind at some point. You should speed up to get back on track, but do so wisely. Don't panic; just take a few seconds less on each question until you're caught up. Don't guess without thinking, but do look through the answer choices and eliminate any you know are wrong. If you can get down to two choices, it is often worthwhile to guess from those. Once you've chosen an answer, move on and don't dwell on any that you skipped or had to hurry through. If a question was taking too long, chances are it was one of the harder ones, so you weren't as likely to get it right anyway.

On the other hand, if you find yourself getting ahead of schedule, it may be beneficial to slow down a little. The more quickly you work, the more likely you are to make a careless mistake that will affect your score. You've budgeted time for each question, so don't be afraid to spend that time. Practice an efficient but careful pace to get the most out of the time you have.

Secret Key #5 – Have a Plan for Guessing

When you're taking the test, you may find yourself stuck on a question. Some of the answer choices seem better than others, but you don't see the one answer choice that is obviously correct. What do you do?

The scenario described above is very common, yet most test takers have not effectively prepared for it. Developing and practicing a plan for guessing may be one of the single most effective uses of your time as you get ready for the exam.

In developing your plan for guessing, there are three questions to address:

- When should you start the guessing process?
- How should you narrow down the choices?
- Which answer should you choose?

When to Start the Guessing Process

Unless your plan for guessing is to select C every time (which, despite its merits, is not what we recommend), you need to leave yourself enough time to apply your answer elimination strategies. Since you have a limited amount of time for each question, that means that if you're going to give yourself the best shot at guessing correctly, you have to decide quickly whether or not you will guess.

Of course, the best-case scenario is that you don't have to guess at all, so first, see if you can answer the question based on your knowledge of the subject and basic reasoning skills. Focus on the key words in the question and try to jog your memory of related topics. Give yourself a chance to bring the knowledge to mind, but once you realize that you don't have (or you can't access) the knowledge you need to answer the question, it's time to start the guessing process.

It's almost always better to start the guessing process too early than too late. It only takes a few seconds to remember something and answer the question from knowledge. Carefully eliminating wrong answer choices takes longer. Plus, going through the process of eliminating answer choices can actually help jog your memory.

Summary: Start the guessing process as soon as you decide that you can't answer the question based on your knowledge.

How to Narrow Down the Choices

The next chapter in this book (**Test-Taking Strategies**) includes a wide range of strategies for how to approach questions and how to look for answer choices to eliminate. You will definitely want to read those carefully, practice them, and figure out which ones work best for you. Here though, we're going to address a mindset rather than a particular strategy.

Your odds of guessing an answer correctly depend on how many options you are choosing from.

Number of options left	5	4	3	2	1
Odds of guessing correctly	20%	25%	33%	50%	100%

You can see from this chart just how valuable it is to be able to eliminate incorrect answers and make an educated guess, but there are two things that many test takers do that cause them to miss out on the benefits of guessing:

- Accidentally eliminating the correct answer
- Selecting an answer based on an impression

We'll look at the first one here, and the second one in the next section.

To avoid accidentally eliminating the correct answer, we recommend a thought exercise called **the $5 challenge**. In this challenge, you only eliminate an answer choice from contention if you are willing to bet $5 on it being wrong. Why $5? Five dollars is a small but not insignificant amount of money. It's an amount you could afford to lose but wouldn't want to throw away. And while losing $5 once might not hurt too much, doing it twenty times will set you back $100. In the same way, each small decision you make—eliminating a choice here, guessing on a question there—won't by itself impact your score very much, but when you put them all together, they can make a big difference. By holding each answer choice elimination decision to a higher standard, you can reduce the risk of accidentally eliminating the correct answer.

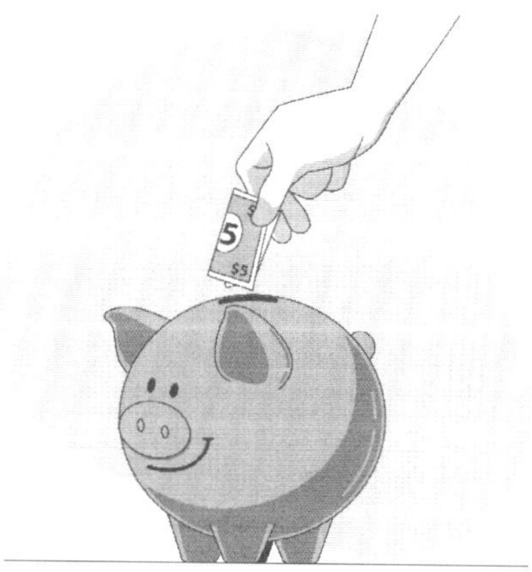

The $5 challenge can also be applied in a positive sense: If you are willing to bet $5 that an answer choice *is* correct, go ahead and mark it as correct.

Summary: Only eliminate an answer choice if you are willing to bet $5 that it is wrong.

Which Answer to Choose

You're taking the test. You've run into a hard question and decided you'll have to guess. You've eliminated all the answer choices you're willing to bet $5 on. Now you have to pick an answer. Why do we even need to talk about this? Why can't you just pick whichever one you feel like when the time comes?

The answer to these questions is that if you don't come into the test with a plan, you'll rely on your impression to select an answer choice, and if you do that, you risk falling into a trap. The test writers know that everyone who takes their test will be guessing on some of the questions, so they intentionally write wrong answer choices to seem plausible. You still have to pick an answer though, and if the wrong answer choices are designed to look right, how can you ever be sure that you're not falling for their trap? The best solution we've found to this dilemma is to take the decision out of your hands entirely. Here is the process we recommend:

Once you've eliminated any choices that you are confident (willing to bet $5) are wrong, select the first remaining choice as your answer.

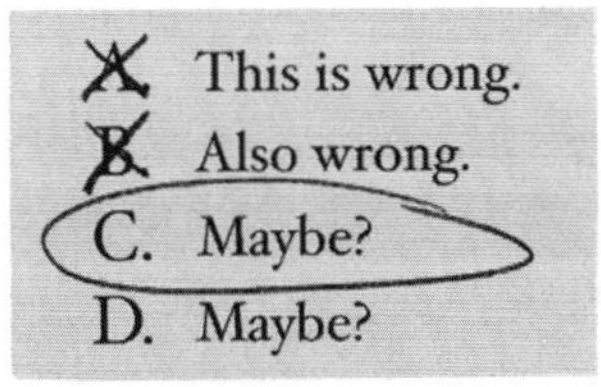

Whether you choose to select the first remaining choice, the second, or the last, the important thing is that you use some preselected standard. Using this approach guarantees that you will not be enticed into selecting an answer choice that looks right, because you are not basing your decision on how the answer choices look.

This is not meant to make you question your knowledge. Instead, it is to help you recognize the difference between your knowledge and your impressions. There's a huge difference between thinking an answer is right because of what you know, and thinking an answer is right because it looks or sounds like it should be right.

Summary: To ensure that your selection is appropriately random, make a predetermined selection from among all answer choices you have not eliminated.

Test-Taking Strategies

This section contains a list of test-taking strategies that you may find helpful as you work through the test. By taking what you know and applying logical thought, you can maximize your chances of answering any question correctly!

It is very important to realize that every question is different and every person is different: no single strategy will work on every question, and no single strategy will work for every person. That's why we've included all of them here, so you can try them out and determine which ones work best for different types of questions and which ones work best for you.

Question Strategies

✓ Read Carefully

Read the question and the answer choices carefully. Don't miss the question because you misread the terms. You have plenty of time to read each question thoroughly and make sure you understand what is being asked. Yet a happy medium must be attained, so don't waste too much time. You must read carefully and efficiently.

✓ Contextual Clues

Look for contextual clues. If the question includes a word you are not familiar with, look at the immediate context for some indication of what the word might mean. Contextual clues can often give you all the information you need to decipher the meaning of an unfamiliar word. Even if you can't determine the meaning, you may be able to narrow down the possibilities enough to make a solid guess at the answer to the question.

✓ Prefixes

If you're having trouble with a word in the question or answer choices, try dissecting it. Take advantage of every clue that the word might include. Prefixes can be a huge help. Usually, they allow you to determine a basic meaning. *Pre-* means before, *post-* means after, *pro-* is positive, *de-* is negative. From prefixes, you can get an idea of the general meaning of the word and try to put it into context.

✓ Hedge Words

Watch out for critical hedge words, such as *likely, may, can, often, almost, mostly, usually, generally, rarely,* and *sometimes*. Question writers insert these hedge phrases to cover every possibility. Often an answer choice will be wrong simply because it leaves no room for exception. Be on guard for answer choices that have definitive words such as *exactly* and *always.*

✓ Switchback Words

Stay alert for *switchbacks*. These are the words and phrases frequently used to alert you to shifts in thought. The most common switchback words are *but, although,* and *however*. Others include *nevertheless, on the other hand, even though, while, in spite of, despite,* and *regardless of.* Switchback words are important to catch because they can change the direction of the question or an answer choice.

⊘ FACE VALUE

When in doubt, use common sense. Accept the situation in the problem at face value. Don't read too much into it. These problems will not require you to make wild assumptions. If you have to go beyond creativity and warp time or space in order to have an answer choice fit the question, then you should move on and consider the other answer choices. These are normal problems rooted in reality. The applicable relationship or explanation may not be readily apparent, but it is there for you to figure out. Use your common sense to interpret anything that isn't clear.

Answer Choice Strategies

⊘ ANSWER SELECTION

The most thorough way to pick an answer choice is to identify and eliminate wrong answers until only one is left, then confirm it is the correct answer. Sometimes an answer choice may immediately seem right, but be careful. The test writers will usually put more than one reasonable answer choice on each question, so take a second to read all of them and make sure that the other choices are not equally obvious. As long as you have time left, it is better to read every answer choice than to pick the first one that looks right without checking the others.

⊘ ANSWER CHOICE FAMILIES

An answer choice family consists of two (in rare cases, three) answer choices that are very similar in construction and cannot all be true at the same time. If you see two answer choices that are direct opposites or parallels, one of them is usually the correct answer. For instance, if one answer choice says that quantity *x* increases and another either says that quantity *x* decreases (opposite) or says that quantity *y* increases (parallel), then those answer choices would fall into the same family. An answer choice that doesn't match the construction of the answer choice family is more likely to be incorrect. Most questions will not have answer choice families, but when they do appear, you should be prepared to recognize them.

⊘ ELIMINATE ANSWERS

Eliminate answer choices as soon as you realize they are wrong, but make sure you consider all possibilities. If you are eliminating answer choices and realize that the last one you are left with is also wrong, don't panic. Start over and consider each choice again. There may be something you missed the first time that you will realize on the second pass.

⊘ AVOID FACT TRAPS

Don't be distracted by an answer choice that is factually true but doesn't answer the question. You are looking for the choice that answers the question. Stay focused on what the question is asking for so you don't accidentally pick an answer that is true but incorrect. Always go back to the question and make sure the answer choice you've selected actually answers the question and is not merely a true statement.

⊘ EXTREME STATEMENTS

In general, you should avoid answers that put forth extreme actions as standard practice or proclaim controversial ideas as established fact. An answer choice that states the "process should be used in certain situations, if..." is much more likely to be correct than one that states the "process should be discontinued completely." The first is a calm rational statement and doesn't even make a definitive, uncompromising stance, using a hedge word *if* to provide wiggle room, whereas the second choice is far more extreme.

⊘ BENCHMARK

As you read through the answer choices and you come across one that seems to answer the question well, mentally select that answer choice. This is not your final answer, but it's the one that will help you evaluate the other answer choices. The one that you selected is your benchmark or standard for judging each of the other answer choices. Every other answer choice must be compared to your benchmark. That choice is correct until proven otherwise by another answer choice beating it. If you find a better answer, then that one becomes your new benchmark. Once you've decided that no other choice answers the question as well as your benchmark, you have your final answer.

⊘ PREDICT THE ANSWER

Before you even start looking at the answer choices, it is often best to try to predict the answer. When you come up with the answer on your own, it is easier to avoid distractions and traps because you will know exactly what to look for. The right answer choice is unlikely to be word-for-word what you came up with, but it should be a close match. Even if you are confident that you have the right answer, you should still take the time to read each option before moving on.

General Strategies

⊘ TOUGH QUESTIONS

If you are stumped on a problem or it appears too hard or too difficult, don't waste time. Move on! Remember though, if you can quickly check for obviously incorrect answer choices, your chances of guessing correctly are greatly improved. Before you completely give up, at least try to knock out a couple of possible answers. Eliminate what you can and then guess at the remaining answer choices before moving on.

⊘ CHECK YOUR WORK

Since you will probably not know every term listed and the answer to every question, it is important that you get credit for the ones that you do know. Don't miss any questions through careless mistakes. If at all possible, try to take a second to look back over your answer selection and make sure you've selected the correct answer choice and haven't made a costly careless mistake (such as marking an answer choice that you didn't mean to mark). This quick double check should more than pay for itself in caught mistakes for the time it costs.

⊘ PACE YOURSELF

It's easy to be overwhelmed when you're looking at a page full of questions; your mind is confused and full of random thoughts, and the clock is ticking down faster than you would like. Calm down and maintain the pace that you have set for yourself. Especially as you get down to the last few minutes of the test, don't let the small numbers on the clock make you panic. As long as you are on track by monitoring your pace, you are guaranteed to have time for each question.

⊘ DON'T RUSH

It is very easy to make errors when you are in a hurry. Maintaining a fast pace in answering questions is pointless if it makes you miss questions that you would have gotten right otherwise. Test writers like to include distracting information and wrong answers that seem right. Taking a little extra time to avoid careless mistakes can make all the difference in your test score. Find a pace that allows you to be confident in the answers that you select.

✓ Keep Moving

Panicking will not help you pass the test, so do your best to stay calm and keep moving. Taking deep breaths and going through the answer elimination steps you practiced can help to break through a stress barrier and keep your pace.

Final Notes

The combination of a solid foundation of content knowledge and the confidence that comes from practicing your plan for applying that knowledge is the key to maximizing your performance on test day. As your foundation of content knowledge is built up and strengthened, you'll find that the strategies included in this chapter become more and more effective in helping you quickly sift through the distractions and traps of the test to isolate the correct answer.

Now that you're preparing to move forward into the test content chapters of this book, be sure to keep your goal in mind. As you read, think about how you will be able to apply this information on the test. If you've already seen sample questions for the test and you have an idea of the question format and style, try to come up with questions of your own that you can answer based on what you're reading. This will give you valuable practice applying your knowledge in the same ways you can expect to on test day.

Good luck and good studying!

History of the United States: 1865 to the Present

American History 1865 to 1898

Hampton Roads Peace Conference, Final Battles, and Assassination of Lincoln

At the Hampton Roads Peace Conference in February of 1865, **Lincoln** and Secretary of State **Seward** met with the vice president of the CSA, **Alexander Stephens**. Lincoln made a stern offer: reunion of the states, emancipation of the slaves, and immediate disbanding of the Confederate army. The Confederates, however, were not yet ready to return to the Union. The Northern General US Grant then led troops toward the CSA capital at Richmond. Finally, at **Appomattox** (VA) in April of 1865, Lee surrendered to Grant. Soon after, the Confederate President **Jefferson Davis** would be caught and jailed. Finally, on April 14, 1865, Lincoln was fatally wounded by two shots from the gun of **John Wilkes Booth** in Ford's Theater in Washington.

Presidential Reconstruction Plan Under Andrew Johnson

Andrew Johnson, a Jacksonian Democrat from Tennessee, became president after the assassination of Lincoln. Though a Southerner, he believed the yeoman farmers of the South had been tricked into war by "cotton snobs." Johnson's plan for reconstruction called for **amnesty** to be granted to all ex-Confederates except for high-ranking officials and wealthy cotton planters, who would be allowed to apply for special pardons. Johnson also called for a **provisional Unionist governor** to be appointed in each Southern state; this leader would hold a constitutional convention at which it would be necessary to disavow secession, repudiate the CSA debt, and accept the 13th amendment. This plan was largely a failure, however, because it infringed on the powers of Congress, was seen as too lenient on the South, threatened the Republicans by giving too much power to Southern Democrats, and ignored freed black people, who were repressed in the South by the so-called **Black Codes**.

Labor Organizations After the Civil War

National Labor Union and Noble and Holy Orders of the Knights of Labor

At the end of the Civil War, only about 2% of all US workers were **unionized**; many believed joining a union was an admission that one would never move up. Over time, though, people began to realize that the consolidation of business interests (trusts) had to be met by a consolidation of labor. In 1866, the **National Labor Union** was founded by William H. Sylvis; this idealistic organization advocated an 8-hour workday but disbanded after backing the loser in the 1872 election. In 1869, Uriah Stephens founded the **Noble and Holy Orders of the Knights of Labor**; this group excluded doctors, lawyers, and bankers and supported the end of sexism, the 8-hour workday, paper money, income tax, and the prohibition of alcohol.

Haymarket Square and American Federation of Labor

In 1886, the **Knights of Labor** gathered in **Haymarket Square** in Chicago to protest an attack against another union. During the protest, a bomb was thrown and several people were killed; 7 members of the union were arrested, and some were executed. This incident linked labor unions with violence in the popular imagination. At the same time, less idealistic labor unions like the American Railway Union (led by Eugene V. Debs), the United Mineworkers, and the Molly McGuires were making great inroads in working communities. The **American Federation of Labor** was an alliance of many unions formed in 1881. This group sought a shorter workday, better working conditions, and workman's compensation; they were also not afraid to strike. The AFL frequently engaged in collective bargaining, in which a strike was threatened in order to bring management to the negotiation table.

Opposition to Organized Labor

The general public **opposed** labor unions because they disliked the idea of closed shops (those places in which one had to be a union member to work) and because they had a reputation for violence. Unions were also fiercely competitive with one another, and there was some animosity between the unions for skilled and unskilled workers. Unions were always at a disadvantage in their dealings with management, in part because management could hire lobbyists (to promote anti-union legislation in Washington) and lawyers and could bribe politicians. Owners often had blacklists of union troublemakers who would not be hired and plenty of "yellow-dog" workers who had signed contracts pledging never to join a union. Owners often hired spies to obtain information among workers, and, in the event of a strike, they could always hire "scabs" to cross the picket lines. It was not unheard of for managers to hire thugs to cause trouble among strikers and perpetuate the rowdy reputation of the unions.

Agricultural Problems During Populism

In the years following the Civil War, the US heartland suffered from an **overabundance** of wheat and rice; these surpluses, coupled with the advances in transportation and communication, drove prices down. Farmers were forced into high debt which they could never repay, leading to **deflation** and a scarcity of currency. Since many farmers didn't own the land that they worked, the banks often had to **foreclose** when farmers were unable to pay their debts. Farmers blamed their problems on a number of different factors. They blamed the railroads, which usually gave discount rates to bigger shippers. They blamed the banks, which loaned money to the rich but were unforgiving of farmers' economic plight. They also blamed the tax system, claiming that it was easy for businesses to hide their assets and impossible for farmers to do so. Additionally, they blamed the tariff, which discouraged other countries from buying US goods.

Early Farm Organization During Populism

The **Patron of Husbandry (Grange)** was founded in 1867 by Oliver Kelley to establish cooperatives, in which individuals bought goods directly from the wholesale distributor. His group was also responsible for the **Granger Laws**, which attacked railroad and grain elevator interests. The Grange had basically disappeared by 1875. The **National Farmer's Alliance and Industrial Union** pursued a number of different initiatives: more national banks, cooperatives, a federal storage system for non-perishable items, more currency, free coinage of silver, reduction of tariffs, direct election of senators, an 8-hour workday, government control of railroads and telegraphs, and one term for the president. This group's success led to the formation of the **Populist Party** in 1890. This party aimed to speak for the farmers and included all of the farmers' unions as well as some labor unions, the Greenbackers, and the Prohibitionists. The party suffered from internal divisions from its inception.

Radical Republican Reconstruction Plan

By 1867, Johnson's Reconstruction plan had largely failed. His unwillingness to change drove many moderate congressmen to become radicals. Radical Republicans came up with their own Reconstruction plan. First, a "Joint Committee of 15" went south to explore the damage done by the war; while there, they discovered the "Black Codes" repressing freed slaves. With the **Civil Rights Act of 1866**, they provided basic rights for ex-slaves (not including the right to vote). The **14th amendment** then gave black people citizenship and said that state governments could not deny anyone life, liberty, and property without due process. This amendment disqualified ex-Confederates from holding public office and declared that states could lose representation if they infringed on the rights of black people. With the **Congressional Reconstruction Act** (Military Reconstruction Act) of 1867, the South was divided into 5 districts and placed under martial law; Congress forced this bill through, and eventually all of the Southern states capitulated.

Review Video: The Reconstruction Era
Visit mometrix.com/academy and enter code: 790561

Tenure of Office Act and the Supreme Court's Activity

The Tenure of Office Act of 1867 established that in order to fire any Cabinet member, the president had to get the approval of the Senate. Though essentially unconstitutional, this act almost ended the presidency of Johnson when he tried to dismiss **Edwin Stanton**, his Secretary of War. Johnson was charged with a crime, **impeached** by the House of Representatives, and missed being impeached by the Senate by one vote. The Supreme Court, though generally quiet during this period, made a couple of significant rulings. In **ex parte Milligan** (1866), the Supreme Court asserted that it is unconstitutional for military rule to continue after regular courts have been reinstated. In **ex parte McCardle** (1868), a similar case, the Supreme Court was too afraid of Congressional radicals to make a ruling.

Radical Republican Reconstruction Governments in the South

Carpetbaggers were Northerners who, under the guise of reinvesting in the Southern economy, took advantage of the situation by acquiring positions in local governments and raising taxes. **Scalawags** were white Republican Southerners who took similar economic advantage. During the rule of the Reconstruction governments, black people were allowed to hold some public offices, though not if they were freed slaves; the black Senator **Hiram Revels** (MS) served in Jefferson Davis' old seat. Black people had very few economic rights and had no land. **Thaddeus Stevens** declared that black people should receive "40 acres and a mule," but nobody was willing to take this land from its present owners. **Sharecropping** became basically another form of slavery. In short, the Reconstruction governments were corrupt, spent too much, levied too many taxes, and took advantage of newly freed slaves. Still, these governments established state constitutions, built roads and schools, and made education compulsory.

Election of 1868 and the Grant Administration

After the Civil War, the US was consumed by **materialism**. The election of 1868 pitted **Ulysses S. Grant** (Republican) against Horatio Seymour (Democrat). Grant was a war hero, and Seymour spent much of the campaign defending himself from allegations that he aided the Confederacy. The Democrats proposed that states should decide for themselves the question of black suffrage, and they wanted to give amnesty to former Confederates. Republicans had much more success with their campaign, blaming the Democrats for the war (a strategy known as "waving the bloody shirt"), and Grant won handily. Grant's presidency would not be as easy as his campaign, however. He had no political experience and was unused to compromise. He frequently fought with his Cabinet, though Secretary of State Hamilton Fish was able to convince him to sign the **Treaty of Washington** (1871), in which Britain compensated the US for aiding the Confederate navy.

Graft and Corruption Under Grant

Crédit Mobilier Scandal, Schuylar Colfax, and Fisk-Gould Scandal

The Grant administration was so corrupt that the president himself had to apologize. One of the most famous fiascos of the era was the **Crédit Mobilier scandal**: the Union Pacific gave a contract to the Crédit Mobilier of America construction company after the federal government secretly loaned Crédit Mobilier of America money for their bid. Then, Vice President **Schuyler Colfax** was caught accepting a bribe in return for ceasing the investigation. In the **Fisk-Gould scandal**, Jim Fisk and Jay Gould convinced Grant to keep government gold out of the New York Stock Exchange, because they hoped to corner the market. Grant became angry with the men and dumped $4 million worth of gold onto the market. September 24, 1869, is known as **Black Friday** on Wall Street; this was the day that Grant's gold flood caused the price of gold to drop so rapidly that the entire market crashed. Gould was able to survive this catastrophe; Fisk was not.

Tammany Hall, Congressional Salary Grab, and Whiskey Ring Scandal

William Marcy "Boss" Tweed was the political boss of New York City. He ran the **Tammany Hall** political machine, a group that fixed elections by recruiting voters with food and jobs. Another instance of corruption under Grant was the **Congressional salary grab**: Congress voted to give themselves a 50% raise, set retroactively by two years. The public was outraged by this avarice, and so, though they kept the pay raise, Congress gave up the back pay. In the **Whiskey ring scandal**, some tax agents who were supposed to be taxing barrels of whiskey were found to have been accepting bribes; this scandal went up as high as Secretary of the Treasury Benjamin Bristow. When historians look at this period and try to figure out why there was so much corruption, they generally decide that it was a carryover from the brutality of the war, combined with the naiveté of the president.

Opposition to Grant and Corruption Under Grant

Thomas Nast was one of the first famous political cartoonists; he made his name satirizing corrupt politicians like Boss Tweed. Grant established the **Civil Service Commission** in 1871, an organization whose mission was to study corruption and make recommendations to the president. Grant paid little attention to this group, however, and it died a quiet death in 1875. During Grant's first term, a group of upper-class Republicans, calling themselves the **Mugwumps**, began to call for a civil service based only on merit. At the same time, the **Liberal Republicans**, another splinter group of the Republican party, spoke out against the graft in civil service, the use of paper money, and the Republican Reconstruction policy. This group supported a lower tariff and better treatment for farmers.

Industrial Era Scandals and Innovations

The infamous **Credit Mobilier scandal** occurred during Grant's presidency in 1872 and involved the Union Pacific Railroad. A more egregious crime was perpetrated on the stockholders of the Erie Railroad; the owners were trying to avoid being bought out by Vanderbilt, and thus they printed up a huge amount of new stock, making it impossible for Vanderbilt to get a majority interest but also vastly diminishing the value of each share. During this era, the following **innovations** and inventors accelerated industry: sleeper cars (George Pullman), air brakes for trains (George Westinghouse), time zones, double tracking (so that two trains could run on the same line), and the standardization of the distance from one rail to another.

Review Video: Industrialization
Visit mometrix.com/academy and enter code: 893924

Election of 1872 and Final Collapse of Grant

In the election of 1872, **Grant** won a second term (over Liberal Republican Horace Greeley) because of his enduring status as a war hero, and because the worst scandals of his administration had yet to be exposed. Quickly, though, Grant's administration fell apart. Five Cabinet members would be found guilty of **corruption**. Then came the **Panic of 1873**. This was the result of three factors: the withdrawal of European investment (Europeans were funneling their money into the Franco-Prussian War), the stock market crash caused by the Fisk-Gould scandal, and the inflexibility of the banks caused by heavy investment in non-liquid assets. As a result of these factors, **Jay Cooke and Co.**, one of the largest banks in the US, collapsed, taking several other banks with it. Eighty-nine railroads soon went under, and then the iron and steel mills had no business. By 1875, half a million Americans were unemployed, and farmers were beginning to lose their land to foreclosure.

Ku Klux Klan and Amnesty Act of 1872

In the 1870s, Southern white people, as members of the Conservatives or Redeemers, began to regain control of the local governments; they sought to do away with "Negro rule." The **Ku Klux Klan** was founded in 1867 by former Confederate General Nathan Bedford Forrest and other ex-Confederates. Though founded as a social club, this group quickly got out of hand, causing the passage of the **Ku Klux Klan and Force Acts** (1870-1), unsuccessful attempts to subdue the Klan by allowing for black militias. The **Amnesty Act of 1872** extended the right to vote to many more ex-Confederates. Gradually, the North began to lose interest in the South for the following reasons: they were disgusted by the corrupt governments, they were frustrated by the persistent racism, and they had agreed to remain distant in exchange for a higher tariff.

Solutions to the Panic of 1873

By 1873, **currency deflation** was a major problem in the US. There were a number of supporters of cheap money, and they encouraged the US government to issue $26 million in greenbacks to stimulate the economy; this plan failed. There was another group of hard-money advocates who suggested using a gold standard, so the government made a compromise called the **Specie Resumption Act of 1875**. This act increased the number of national banks in the South and West, allowed national banks to issue as many notes as they wanted (up to a $300 million limit), and named a "day of redemption," on which all greenbacks could be exchanged for gold coins. The day of redemption never came to pass, however, which seemed to be a victory for the cheap money supporters. Instead, it became evident that the promise of gold exchange caused the public to treat greenbacks as if they were "good as gold." By 1879, the economy was back on track and the Republicans had acquired the reputation as the party in favor of business.

Subordination of Western Native Americans Until 1874

The Native Americans who roamed the Great Plains were known as fierce hunters, and there were a few bloody encounters between settlers heading west and the natives. In 1851, the US established the **Concentration policy**, which encouraged Native Americans to live close to one another. This strategy was untenable, however, and the period from 1860-90 was marked by frequent conflict. In the **Sioux Wars** of 1865-7, the Sioux were led by **Red Cloud**; they fought and lost to American troops after their sacred hunting ground was mined. For a while, the US tried to group tribes on reservations in Oklahoma and the Black Hills; from 1869-74, Generals Sherman and Sheridan engaged in a **War of Extermination** to kill those who refused to move.

Subordination of the Western Native Americans from 1875-1887

According to **Grant's Peace Program**, each Native American tribe would be put under the control of different religious groups. In 1875, miners were allowed back into the Black Hills, prompting the **Sioux War** of 1875-6, during which Sitting Bull defeated Custer at the **Battle of Little Big Horn**. Around this time, Chief Joseph attempted to lead his Nez Perce tribe to Canada; this mission failed and the Nez Perce were sent to Oklahoma. The Apache leader Geronimo was defeated in Arizona in 1887. At the **Battle of Wounded Knee**, the US army massacred 300, mostly women and children. Native Americans were doomed by their inferior weapons; by the destruction by white people of their food supply, the buffalo; and by railroads which made it easier for white people to encroach on their hunting grounds.

Election of 1876 and National Self-Evaluation

The election of 1876, won by **Rutherford B. Hayes** (Republican) over Samuel J. Tilden (Democrat), coincided with the **US centennial**, so people were compelled to consider the history of the country thus far. When Americans of 1876 looked back, they had some reason to be pleased: they had survived a Civil War intact and had witnessed the end of slavery. They also had developed a strong national government. On the other hand, many Americans were disillusioned at this time by the scandals of the Grant administration. There had also been violent and disheartening struggles between black militiamen and the Ku Klux Klan in the South. Finally, many in the country were still reeling from Custer's bloody defeat at the Battle of Little Big Horn.

Election of 1876 and Compromise of 1877

In 1876, **Rutherford B. Hayes** (Republican) defeated Samuel Tilden (Democrat) after an electoral commission composed mostly of Republicans ruled that certain votes by carpetbag governments should have gone to him. As part of the ensuing **Compromise of 1877**, the South was given federal money for improvements to infrastructure, a Southerner was placed in Hayes' Cabinet, and the Union troops propping up the carpetbag governments were removed. This election established the tradition of the "**Solid South**": it was assumed that every year the majority of Southerners would vote for the Democratic candidate.

Hayes Presidency

Highlights

Foolishly, **Rutherford B. Hayes** made himself a lame-duck president by announcing soon after taking office that he would not seek a second term. Hayes' wife was nicknamed "Lemonade Lucy," because she would not allow any alcohol in the White House. Hayes tried to restore the power of the presidency after the debacle of Grant, but he was weakened by intense struggles over his Cabinet confirmations. One thing Hayes can be credited with is making a gallant attempt to destroy the **spoils system**. He replaced the Collector of the Customs House after discovering the corruption of that body, and he appointed Carl Schurz Secretary of the Interior on the basis of merit. In turn, Schurz established a merit system in his department, creating an entrance exam for potential employees.

Low-Points

One of the failures of the Hayes administration was its handling of the **Great Rail Strike of 1877**. When over two-thirds of the rail lines were shut down by strikes, Hayes sent in federal troops, and there was considerable bloodshed. This set a bad precedent for how strikes would be handled in the future. Hayes vetoed an attempt by western labor unions to restrict Chinese immigration, saying that this would be a violation of the **Burlingame Treaty**. One of the main issues in the Hayes years was monetary policy. Farmers, who were often in debt, wanted a soft currency not backed by anything; they were willing to settle for a silver standard. In **Hepburn v. Griswold** (1869), the Supreme Court had ruled that there could not be paper money without a gold standard; in the **Legal Tender cases of 1871**, however, the Court reversed itself. The bickering over these conflicting rulings plagued the Hayes administration.

Hayes vs. Greenbackers and the Silverites

After the **Specie Resumption Act of 1875**, Hayes worked to minimize the effects of the oncoming "day of redemption," in which paper money could be exchanged for gold coins. He began a policy of contraction, wherein the government gradually took in paper money and issued gold, and he funded attempts to mine more gold. The **Greenbackers** were those who wanted Hayes to postpone the day of redemption; he did not, and it ultimately proved anticlimactic, as people assumed their paper money was "good as gold" and didn't bother to redeem it. Hayes also had to deal with the **Silverites**. In 1873, the government had enraged silver prospectors by announcing that it would no longer make coins out of silver. In answer to their fury, Hayes pushed through the **Bland-Allison Act**, which established that a minimum of $2 million of silver had to be purchased and coined by the government every month.

Competition and Disorder in the Industrial Era

The late 19th century was marked by intense competition between the railroads. Railroads offered secret illegal refunds to big customers, and in areas where they had no competition, they charged exorbitant prices. After the 1870s, various states tried to tame the railroads; one such instance of this kind of regulation was the **Granger Laws**. Farmers often felt that they were charged more than others. In **Munn v. Illinois** (1877), the Supreme Court asserted that the state governments had the right to regulate the railroads. In Wabash, St. Louis, and **Pacific Railroad Co. v. Illinois** (1886), the Supreme Court reversed its former opinion and declared that only the federal government could regulate the railroads. Finally, with the **Interstate Commerce Act of 1887**, the federal government forbade discriminatory practices like refunds and price-fixing; unfortunately, these laws were rarely enforced.

Great Strike of 1877, the Homestead Strike, and the Pullman Strike

The Great Strike of 1877 occurred in West Virginia when state police and militiamen were sent to break up a railway strike and joined it instead. President Hayes sent in the army, and at least 100 people were killed breaking up the strike. This debacle set a bad precedent for future strikes. In the **Homestead (PA) Strike** of July 1892, a group of soldiers called by Henry Clay Frick (temporarily in charge of one of Carnegie's steel mills) brutally broke up a strike. In 1894, a group of **Pullman railcar employees** began a strike, supported by the American Railway Union of Eugene V. Debs. All rail workers then went on strike out of sympathy for the Pullman workers. The rail owners got an injunction, claiming that the rail workers were interfering with interstate trade and therefore violating the **Sherman Anti-trust Act**. This did not end the strike, and thus President Grover Cleveland had to send in the army under the false premise that the strike was holding up the US mail.

Election of 1880

In the election of 1880, the **Republican party** was beset by internal squabbling between the stalwarts and half-breeds over the issue of patronage. This led to a chaotic nominating convention in which a campaign manager, **James A. Garfield**, became the candidate. Garfield won a narrow victory over the Democrat Winfield Scott Hancock, a war hero with no political experience. Garfield was a charismatic figure whose administration began with a successful compromise among Republicans; unfortunately, he was shot and killed in 1881. Garfield was succeeded by his vice-president, **Chester A. Arthur**. The major event of his presidency was the **Civil Service Act of 1883**, which established a commission to create competitive examinations for potential government employees. Arthur also helped create the modern US navy.

New South in the 1880s

In the 1880s, the old Southern plantations began to break up, in part because the high taxes imposed by the new governments made them unprofitable. The land was mainly worked by tenant farmers and sharecroppers: **tenant farmers** worked and paid rent on someone else's land, while **sharecroppers** worked the whole plantation and got a share of the crop. Tenant farmers were mostly poor white people, while sharecroppers were mostly freed black people. There was considerable diversification in agriculture around this time, brought on not only by innovation (cotton picker, tractor), but by the **Morrill Land Grant Act**, which gave grants for the creation of agricultural colleges. Clarence Birdseye's development of the refrigerated railroad car spurred farming as well. Also, as the road and rail infrastructure improved in the South, so did Southern industry.

GILDED AGE

CHARACTERISTICS

The period in American history between Reconstruction and the Progressive Era is commonly known as the **Gilded Age**. During this period, the US seemed to be simultaneously abandoning the ideals of the past and failing to anticipate the future; this was in large part due to the confusion of a horrendous Civil War and massive immigration, industrialization, and urbanization. During this period, many Americans sought refuge in **community organizations** like the Moose Lodge, the Elks Club, and the Masonic Lodge. The politicians of the Gilded Age tended to avoid the major issues of **social injustice and inequality**, instead focusing on minor issues like public v. parochial schools, and the blue laws (laws restricting commercial activity on Sunday).

Review Video: The Gilded Age: An Overview
Visit mometrix.com/academy and enter code: 684770

POLITICS

Although the **Republicans** dominated the executive branch during the Gilded Age, Congress was evenly divided. The Republican party was composed mainly of people from the Northeast and Midwest. Black people typically were Republicans (that is, when they were allowed into the political process). In general, the Republicans supported high tariffs and sound money. One of the main internal disputes in the Republican party was between the **stalwarts**, who supported the spoils system, and the **half-breeds**, who did not. As for the **Democrats**, they were largely based in the South or in the big cities of the North. The Democrats and Republicans butted heads over ethnic, religious, and cultural issues, but they tended to avoid larger economic and social issues. Extremely talented individuals were more likely to go into business than politics during this era. Another trend of the Gilded Age was the domination of the president by Congress.

AMERICAN LABOR IN THE GILDED AGE

As the US emerged from the Civil War, one of the main economic problems was that most workers were **unskilled**. In general, working conditions were horrendous and wages were low. There was little homogeneity in the labor force, either, making it difficult for workers to switch jobs. **Immigrants** were usually willing to take more dangerous jobs than natives; during the 1880s, more than 5 million immigrants entered the US. In 1882, the **Chinese Exclusion Act** put a 10-year moratorium on Chinese immigration. In 1885, the **Foran Act** prohibited American businessmen from traveling to China to recruit workers. Both of these acts were open violations of the **Burlingame Treaty of 1868**, which had provided for open Chinese immigration.

SOCIAL CRITICS AND DISSENTERS IN THE GILDED AGE

In his book *Dynamic Sociology*, **Lester Frank Ward** railed against the Social Darwinism espoused by the upper class; he declared that humans were more than mere animals. In *Progress and Poverty*, **Henry George** asserted that poverty was the result of poor legislation rather than any inherent weakness in the poor. **Edward Bellamy** promoted socialism in his novel *Looking Back* (1888); in it, a man of the year 2000 describes how America was turned into a utopian society through the abolition of corporations. Also, at this time, **Thorstein Veblen** exposed the phenomenon of "conspicuous consumption" in his *Theory of the Leisure Class*. All of these critics were disgusted by the hypocrisy of the **robber barons**; these magnates claimed to support laissez-faire government, yet they wanted high tariffs to protect their businesses.

Laissez-Faire Conservatism and the Gospel of Wealth

The so-called "**Gilded Age**" of American history, which ran roughly from 1880 to 1900, only looked prosperous from a distance. Many at this time believed that wealth justified itself and that God showed his favor in people by making them rich. Many business leaders did not trust politicians because they did not feel that they had had to fight their way to the top. Businessmen believed that the role of the government was to protect property and trade through tariffs. **William Graham Sumner** wrote the essay "What the Social Classes Owe Each Other," in which he declared that corporations shouldn't demand high tariff rates, but the government shouldn't respond to requests to clean up the slums. There was a general sense that the poor were responsible for their plight. Around this time, the popular imagination was inspired by the rags-to-riches fables of **Horatio Alger**.

Redeemers

The Redeemers sought to prevent black people from voting and to return power to the "natural leaders." In response, the **Populist party** was formed; it was an uneasy alliance of black people and poor white people. Southern Democrats tried to exploit the tension within the Populist party. In order to keep black people from voting, Democrats subjected voters to literacy tests, property tests, criminal background checks, residency requirements, and the so-called **Grandfather Clause**, which stated that individuals could not vote unless their ancestors had voted before January 1, 1867. These restrictions, known collectively as the **Mississippi Plan**, were upheld by the Supreme Court, which ruled in **Williams v. Mississippi** (1898) that they were legal because they never explicitly stated that black people could not vote.

Black Southerners and Segregation

Most Southern Democrats supported **segregation**, or the separation of the races. Although the **Civil Rights Act of 1875** had outlawed segregated restaurants and hotels, among other things, the Supreme Court ruled in 1883 that this act violated the 14th amendment because only states, and not individuals, could be forbidden from segregation. The **Jim Crow laws** were those rules that segregated black people and white people. Although de facto (by custom) segregation had existed in the North for years, the South began to implement segregation de jure (by law). In **Plessy v. Ferguson** (1896), the Supreme Court ruled that accommodations should be "separate but equal." In **Cummings v. Board of Education** (1898), the Supreme Court allowed public schools to be segregated.

Booker T. Washington and W.E.B. DuBois

Booker T. Washington was an ex-slave who founded the Tuskegee Institute in 1881; he felt that black people should establish economic independence before worrying about political rights. In his **Atlanta Exposition speech**, he declared that black people needed to humble themselves to white people. Professor **W.E.B. DuBois** attacked Washington's speech as a compromise; DuBois believed black people should take everything they were due. In 1914, both Washington and DuBois met with Marcus Garvey, who believed that black people should return to Africa and establish a separate country (interestingly, most of Garvey's financial support came from the KKK). At around this time, Paul Laurence Dunbar was achieving renown as the "poet laureate of the Negro race," and Charles Waddell Chestnut was admired as a popular black novelist.

Election of 1884

In 1884, the incumbent Arthur was passed over by his party in favor of Secretary of State James G. Blaine. This proved to be a bad move, as the **Democratic** candidate, **Grover Cleveland**, was able to win the support of conservative Republicans (Mugwumps) and claim a narrow victory. The highlights of the Cleveland administration include the further reform of civil service and the government's successful stand against ex-Union soldiers who were protesting for large pensions. Cleveland reluctantly signed the **Interstate Commerce Act**, and he was correct in predicting that it would not be enforced. Cleveland also spent a great deal of time on tariffs: he attempted to reduce the overall duty with the **Mongrel Tariff** and the **Mills Bill of 1888**, neither of which were very successful.

Solutions to the "Indian Problem"

The US government constructed several policies in an attempt to solve the so-called "**Indian Problem**." The **Dawes (Severalty) Act of 1887** asserted that Natives needed to be assimilated into American society; tribes were moved onto "allotments of severalty" (reservations), which they supposedly owned, although they had no control of the land. The **Indian Reorganization (Howard-Wheeler) Act of 1934** encouraged a return to tribal life and offered Natives money for college. In 1953, with the so-called "**termination policy**," Natives became the responsibility of the states rather than the federal government. In 1970, the new strategy was "self-determination without termination": Natives were allowed to move where they choose and were promised money (which they did not receive).

Election of 1888

In 1888, the Republican **Benjamin Harrison** narrowly upset the incumbent Cleveland, despite having less of the popular vote. Harrison did not accomplish much civil service reform and spent a great deal of time managing insubordination in Congress. Harrison's Republican agenda promoted the **Federal Election Bill**, which was a response to the Mississippi Plan designed to protect the voting rights of freedmen. The **Silver Purchase Bill** was favored by the west but lacked the votes to get through. In the **Compromise of 1890**, the Western Republicans got the silver purchase (Sherman Silver Purchase Act), Southern Democrats got the defeat of the Federal Election Bill, and the Northern Republicans got a higher tariff (McKinley Tariff of 1890). Harrison's administration became known for giving money away for virtually any reason: pensions were excessive, the silver purchase cost federal money, and all of the income tax taken during the Civil War was given back to the people.

Election of 1892 and the Panic of 1893

Grover Cleveland (Dem) defeated Benjamin Harrison (Rep) in the election of 1892 primarily because of his financial conservatism, his promise to change the tariff, and Harrison's weakened state following the epidemic of strikes in 1892. Then came the **Panic of 1893**, caused by labor troubles, over-speculation in the railroads, and an agricultural depression. First, the Philadelphia and Reading Railroads collapsed, then the stock markets collapsed, then the banks folded, draining the gold reserves, then the other railroads folded, and finally the factories were forced to close. Cleveland believed that the cause of this Panic was the **Sherman Silver Purchase Act**, so he repealed it. This plan did absolutely nothing financially, and it split the Democratic party politically.

Panic of 1893 and Domestic Affairs Under Cleveland

After the Panic of 1893, a group known as the **Silverite school** declared that the economic problems could be solved if the US would begin coining silver again. Cleveland, however, ignored this advice and elected to buy gold with the profits from the sale of government bonds. This strategy was somewhat successful. It was during the **Panic of 1893** that the suggestion to battle economic depression by employing people on public works was first made. One of Cleveland's major policy moves in his second term was the **Wilson-Gorman Tariff of 1894**. This lowered the tariff rate and established trade with Latin America. It also established a small income tax on wealthy individuals, though this income tax would be repealed in the **Supreme Court case Pollock v. Farmer's Loan and Trust** (1895). Cleveland's last term was diminished by ineffective enforcement of the **Sherman Anti-trust Act** and the **Interstate Commerce Act**.

J.P. Morgan and Banker Control

The **Panic of 1893** was brought on by the collapse of the **Philadelphia and Reading Railroads**; soon after, 192 railroads failed. In a panic, railroad magnates turned to bankers, especially the "Railroad Doctor," **J.P. Morgan**. Morgan insisted that all of the business' records be opened to him. His usual strategy was to encourage old investors to reinvest; to sell more, "watered-down" stock; and to place either himself or one of his associates on the Board of Directors. In this way, Morgan was able to create a set of "interlocking directories," conglomerations of businesses in which he had an interest. He created many large companies this way, among them General Electric, Western Union, and Equitable.

Andrew Carnegie and Steel

The potential for making money in **steel** was made possible by the development of the **Bessemer process**, whereby iron ore was converted into wrought iron and then had its impurities removed with cold air. **Andrew Carnegie**, an immigrant from Scotland who rose to the top of the Pennsylvania Railroad, was one of the first to make his fortune in steel. He was not especially knowledgeable about steel, but he was the first manager to make a point of **vertical integration**; that is, control of every step of the production process. Carnegie bought out most of his competitors, until he was eventually bought out by J.P. Morgan. Carnegie and his fellows believed in a sort of "gospel of wealth," the idea that they had risen to the top through a process like natural selection. They also believed in using their money for the community.

Review Video: Andrew Carnegie and the Steel Industry
Visit mometrix.com/academy and enter code: 696753

John D. Rockefeller and the Trust

John D. Rockefeller came from a working-class background but gradually rose to become the owner of the wildly profitable **Standard Oil company**. Rockefeller was known for spying on his competitors and intimidating his employees. In 1870, Standard allied itself with 40 other companies; when this alliance began, the group controlled 10% of the market, but by 1881 they controlled almost 95%. In 1882, Standard Oil created a **trust**: alliance members gave their stock to Standard in exchange for trust certificates. The federal government began to get suspicious of these powerful trusts, and in 1890 the **Sherman Anti-trust Act** was passed. This act forbade trusts, but it was worded so vaguely that it was ineffective. In the case of **US v. E.C. Knight Co.** (1895), the Supreme Court ruled that the Knight sugar refinery was not a monopoly because it didn't hurt interstate trade; businesses saw this ruling as a call to monopolize.

Republican Ascendancy in the Election of 1896

The Republicans had been successful in the Congressional elections of 1894, and they nominated **William McKinley** for president in 1896. McKinley was in favor of high tariffs and the gold standard. He was opposed by William Jennings Bryan of the Democrats. McKinley had a wealth of political experience and money, and the Democrats were blamed by many for the economic depression under Cleveland; McKinley won fairly easily. This election marked a 36-year period of domination by the **Republicans**. It also spelled the end of the Populist party. Around this time, gold was found in the Yukon, lending credence to the Republican belief in the gold standard.

IMPERIALISM

DURING THE PERIOD OF WITHDRAWAL (CIVIL WAR TO 1880S)

In the period after the Civil War, the US for the most part withdrew from **foreign affairs**. The Secretaries of State in this period, however, were very aggressive: **Seward** interfered in Korean politics, tried to assert influence in the Caribbean, and famously purchased Alaska from Russia in 1867 for $7.2 million. **Hamilton Fish** tried and failed to annex Santo Domingo. Aside from these instances, though, the US kept its distance. For the most part, this was because it was preoccupied with its own problems. There was also a common belief that invading and colonizing other countries would be a violation of the US **Declaration of Independence**. Many were remembering Washington's farewell address, in which he advised the US to avoid military entanglements, and others were wary of violating the **Monroe Doctrine**.

DURING THE NEW MANIFEST DESTINY (1880S TO 1920S)

In the 1880s, the US began to take a stronger interest in **foreign affairs**. This was in part due to humanitarian concern; the US felt it could improve the standard of living around the world. There was also, of course, an economic motive; manufacturers wanted to find a new source of raw materials, as well as a new market for their products. Missionaries began to travel abroad in this period, trying to convert foreigners to Christianity. There were also military reasons for the increased activity abroad; the US decided it would be a good idea to acquire naval bases in the Pacific, and a group known as the **Jingoists** openly looked for a military conflict. Theodore Roosevelt and Henry Cabot Lodge were both Jingoists.

BERING SEA, PAN-AMERICAN UNION, AND SAMOAN ISLANDS CONFLICT

The "**Seal Battle**" was fought in the Bering Sea between British Canada and the US mainly over boundary lines. In 1893, the two sides met and established mutual boundaries between Alaska and Canada. In 1889, the first meeting of the **Pan-American Union** was held in Washington, DC. In 1878, the US had established a naval base at Pago Pago. Both the British and Germans demanded access to the base. In 1889, the US allowed both the British and Germans to jointly occupy the base. In 1899, the **Samoan islands** were divided up among the US and the European powers.

CONFLICT WITH ITALY, BALTIMORE INCIDENT, BOUNDARY DISPUTES IN SOUTH AMERICA, AND HAWAII

Between the years 1889 and 1891, the US came into conflict with **Italy** after members of the **Sicilian Black Hand**, a terrorist group, were lynched without just cause in New Orleans. The US also sparred with Chile after 2 sailors from the ***USS Baltimore*** died during a bar fight in Valparaiso, Chile. At around this time, a boundary dispute erupted between **British Guiana** and **Venezuela** after gold was discovered in the vaguely defined border region. Britain was ready to send troops into South America, but the US dissuaded them from doing so, citing the Monroe Doctrine. Meanwhile, all throughout the 19th century, the US had been closing in on a conquest of **Hawaii**. After New England missionaries stumbled upon the islands, the US had gotten the natives to sign trade treaties with various US companies. In the 1890s, the US army, led by pineapple magnate Sanford Dole, ousted the native leadership. Hawaii was annexed by the US in 1898.

Review Video: An Overview of American Imperialism
Visit mometrix.com/academy and enter code: 629170

SPANISH-AMERICAN WAR

CAUSES

The **Spanish-American War** centered around **Cuba**. There had already been several revolts against the Spanish leadership on that island, and the **Wilson-Gorman Tariff** had damaged the Cuban economy. In 1896, the Spanish sent General Valeriano Weyler to establish a reconcentration camp, where the dissenting Cubans could be weeded out. Many in the United States pushed the government to intervene in Cuba; businessmen were worried about their crops, Christians and humanitarians were worried about the Cuban people, and imperialists saw a good chance to seize the island. The two final causes of the war were the **DeLome letter**, in which the Spanish minister to the US insulted President McKinley, and the explosion of the ***USS Maine*** in Havana Harbor. Although the Spanish still claim to not have caused this explosion, the US nevertheless declared war on April 25, 1898.

OVERVIEW

The Spanish-American War only lasted between six and eight weeks before the US claimed victory. The first phase of it was fought in the Philippines and the second in Cuba. In Cuba, the United States scored a crucial victory when a rag-tag group of soldiers known as the **Roughriders** (Theodore Roosevelt among them) took Kettle Hill and secured Santiago. Although the **Teller Amendment of 1898** had promised independence to Cuba after the war, the **Platt Amendment**, which was inserted into the Cuban Constitution in 1901, made Cuba a protectorate of the US. The US control of **Guantanamo Bay** dates back to this amendment. In 1934, Cuba received its independence. The Spanish-American War formally ended with the signing of the **Treaty of Paris** in 1898. The US received Guam, the Philippines, Puerto Rico, Cuba, and Wake Island. The US also paid the Spanish $20 million because Manila had supposedly surrendered after the end of the war, making it an invalid wartime concession.

DEBATE OVER THE PHILIPPINES AND THE FILIPINO WAR

In the years 1898 and 1899, the question of what to do about the **Philippines** was hotly debated in the US. **Imperialists** (including Henry Cabot Lodge and Theodore Roosevelt), wanted to make the group of islands into a state, argued against **Anti-imperialists** (e.g., Andrew Carnegie, Mark Twain) who felt that the US would be drawn into Asian conflicts. Some politicians, like William Jennings Bryan, voted for the Treaty of Paris and the acquisition of the Philippines because they felt it would be a disaster that would discourage further imperialism. In 1899, the Filipino leader **Aguinaldo** led the people against US forces. This uprising was only crushed after much cruelty. Later, the **Tydings-McDuffie Act of 1934** promised independence to the Philippines within 10 years but they did not receive it until 1946. Some relevant Supreme Court rulings from this period were in the **Insular Cases of 1901**: the Court asserted that citizens of US territories do not have the same rights as citizens of the continental US.

American History 1899 to the Present

John Hay's Defense of China

From 1898 to 1905, **John Hay** was the Secretary of State. One of his great achievements was establishing the **Open Door Policy** with respect to China. China had just been defeated by Japan and was in the process of being carved up by the European powers into various spheres of economic influence. Hay asserted that each nation should allow equal access for all nations and should respect the rights of the Chinese. Somewhat surprisingly, Europe agreed to this policy of goodwill. The Open Door Policy did not, however, keep China from being exploited by foreign traders. In the **Boxer Rebellion of 1900**, the Chinese rose up against foreigners and were promptly routed by an international coalition (including the US).

Election of 1900 and Theodore Roosevelt

In the election of 1900, **McKinley** and Theodore Roosevelt of the Republicans defeated William Jennings Bryan of the Democrats. McKinley was then assassinated on September 6, 1901, and **Roosevelt** took over. Roosevelt is known as a follower of the African proverb, "Speak softly and carry a big stick." He was known for having very little respect for the system of checks and balances. If the Constitution were too rigid on an issue for his tastes, he ignored it; if Congress acted up, he would subdue them with a mixture of compromise and coercion. Roosevelt displayed his blunt skill in diplomacy in the **Alaska Panhandle dispute of 1903** (in which he decided which islands the US would get, and which would belong to the British) and in the **Morocco Dispute of 1905**, in which he (along with Britain and France) dissuaded Germany from trying to take the North African country.

Panama Canal

Beginnings Under Roosevelt

The Spanish-American War had demonstrated that the US needed a **Latin American canal** in order to become a major naval power. At that time, however, their hands were tied by the **Clayton-Bulwer Treaty of 1850**, which had stated that neither the US nor Britain would build a canal in Latin America without the other. Fortunately for the US, the British were distracted by the Boer War in South Africa and thus were willing to sign the **Hay-Pauncefote Treaty** in 1901, allowing the US to go it alone. Many in the US, including Roosevelt, wanted to build the canal in Nicaragua because it has a number of lakes that could be connected, and because it is mostly flat. Others lobbied for Panama, pointing out that a French contractor had already started work on a canal there and that Panama was narrower than Nicaragua.

Organization Required to Build

In 1902, the United States struck a deal with a Panamanian builder for the control of the canal project. The US then needed to acquire the land. Panama at this time was owned by Colombia; the Colombians rejected the first offer made by the US, leading Roosevelt to call them "blackmailers." Then, in 1903, a rebellion broke out in Panama; Roosevelt recognized the new, independent country after less than a day of fighting. Fifteen days later, the US purchased the **Panama Canal Zone** from the new foreign minister for $10 million initially and $250,000 per year. Many observers were embarrassed by the deal the United States had won from a fledgling country. Nevertheless, Roosevelt then hired engineer John Stephens to finish the job.

Building and Opening

Once Roosevelt finally secured the building supplies and the land to construct the Panama Canal, the brutal and dangerous work began. In order to prevent malaria, the US paved streets, drained swamps, and built houses so that the workers would not have to sleep in tents. Nevertheless, the workdays were long and the pay was low. In the end, the canal cost about $400 million; it was finished in 1913 but did not open until the next year. Roosevelt's visit to Panama made him the first president to leave the US during his term. In 1920, a guilty Democratic Congress gave Colombia $25 million. At present, about 12,000 ships go through the canal every year, and it takes about 8 hours to get from one end to the other.

Roosevelt and the 2nd Venezuelan Crisis

In 1902, many Latin American countries were deep in debt to Europe and were not making any moves to repay their debts. Enraged, European countries began to use military force. At first, Roosevelt supported this policy, but he gradually changed his mind, in part because the American public was opposed to it. When Germany, therefore, sent ships to Santo Domingo in 1904, Roosevelt announced the **Roosevelt Corollary** to the Monroe Doctrine. This document stated that nations may not use force to collect debts. Roosevelt asserted that the US would peaceably arbitrate these disputes before Europe could get violent; he felt these interventions would help Latin America and prevent European recolonization. The US developed a reputation as "the policeman of the Caribbean."

Roosevelt Republicans and Roosevelt as a "Trustbuster"

For Roosevelt Republicans, the principles of good **domestic policy** could be summed up as the "3 Cs": control of the corporations, consumer protection, and the conservation of natural resources. Roosevelt had made his name as a member of the **Roughriders** in the Spanish-American War. Interestingly, his presidency was a result of his unpopularity in his own party: his fellow Republicans had nominated him as vice president because this was felt to be a weak position. They were of course quite displeased when McKinley was assassinated and Roosevelt became president. Roosevelt quickly became famous for his attacks on the trusts. He went after the **Northern Securities Company**, run by, among others, J. P. Morgan and John D. Rockefeller. Morgan attempted to bribe Attorney General Philip Knox to halt the investigation; Knox promptly reported this to Roosevelt. In all, 44 **anti-trust cases** were heard during Roosevelt's presidency.

Roosevelt's Square Deal

Roosevelt's Square Deal was a domestic agenda designed to help the working class and diminish the power of the corporations. The **Elkins Act** made railroad rebates illegal, making it difficult for preferential treatment to be given to corporations. Roosevelt formed the **Department of Commerce and Labor** to help workers. One telling episode was the **Anthracite Coal Strike** in 1902. When the owner of the mines asked Roosevelt for an injunction forcing the employees back to work, Roosevelt instead sent troops in to mine the coal for the government! The owner and the labor leader then met at the White House to settle their differences. This was the first time both sides in a strike had accepted an executive commission, and the first time the president had threatened to seize property. It was also the first time a president had sided with a labor union.

Election of 1904

In the election of 1904, Roosevelt used the **Square Deal** as his platform and was able to defeat the Democrat Judge Alton B. Parker. As part of the Square Deal, Roosevelt mandated an **open shop policy**; workers would be free to join a union without being obliged to do so. A case in which Roosevelt's government did not benefit workers was the **Danbury Hatters' Strike**. During this dispute, the workers organized a general boycott of Danbury Hats. The management argued that this boycott violated the **Sherman Anti-trust Act** and the **Interstate Commerce Act**, and the Supreme Court agreed. Many workers blamed Roosevelt for this decision.

Roosevelt's Reforms

The **Hepburn Act of 1906** gave the ICC the authority to set shipping prices in the event that a shipper complained about the rates. This act also allowed the government to regulate pipelines and express and sleeping car companies. The **Pure Food and Drug Act of 1906** established the Food and Drug Administration to regulate what had become a very corrupt industry. The **Meat Inspection Act of 1906** was inspired by Upton Sinclair's novel *The Jungle*, which exposed the corruption of the meatpacking industry. It established tougher regulation of meat handlers. Not all of Roosevelt's legislation passed, however. He was unable to pass laws against child labor, establish a national worker's compensation, or restrict the power of the **National Association of Manufacturers** to gain injunctions against strikers.

Roosevelt's New Programs and the Old Guard Republicans

Many Old Guard Republicans disagreed with Theodore Roosevelt on the issue of resource conservation. The **Newlands Reclamation Act of 1902** tried to reclaim the wilderness through the construction of dams. Roosevelt believed that the United States only had about a quarter of its original trees; this act set aside land in the Grand Canyon, Yosemite, and Yellowstone for the preservation of forests. Roosevelt also had to endure the **Panic of 1907**, which was caused by too much supply, a decrease in demand, and a short money supply resulting from a lack of gold. The **Aldrich-Vreeland Act of 1908** authorized national banks to issue emergency currency. Over time, it seemed that Roosevelt had become more radical. The **Employers Liability Act of 1906**, for instance, had provided for workman's compensation but was struck down by the courts. Roosevelt promptly went after the courts.

Second Hague Disarmament Conference, Treaty of Portsmouth, Japanese Laborers, and Great White Fleet

At the Second Hague Disarmament Conference in 1907, a number of nations gathered to reaffirm the **Hague Conference rules** of humane warfare and agreed upon how the collection of debts should be pursued. After the **Russo-Japanese War**, Roosevelt rather reluctantly agreed to mediate between the two countries. The result was the **Treaty of Portsmouth**, in which the Japanese lost some land (though not as much as the Russians felt was appropriate). For this, Roosevelt received the 1906 **Nobel Peace Prize**. After the Russo-Japanese War, many **Japanese workers** came to the US; Roosevelt had to intervene and prevent them from being discriminated against. Finally, Roosevelt promoted the **US Navy** by painting a number of ships white and parading them past the Asian coast.

Review Video: The Treaty of Portsmouth
Visit mometrix.com/academy and enter code: 566070

Progressive Movement

Demographic Trends and Working Class

The **Progressive Movement** was marked by advances in rights for workers, women, and minorities. As the 20th century began, it seemed as if the rich were getting richer and the poor were becoming more numerous. Per capita income and population had both increased dramatically, but wealth seemed to be concentrated in a smaller and smaller group. Between one-third and one-half of all factory workers lived in poverty and management showed no concern for these workers in the form of unemployment or worker's compensation. Many of the wealthy magnates felt the poor were that way because of their sinfulness and thus had no desire to provide aid. At the same time, many in the middle class feared that the lower class would revolt, although they didn't want to cause trouble themselves.

Labor Unions, Immigrants, and Black People

By 1914 the **American Federation of Labor** had 2 million members, although most Americans still did not trust labor unions. Meanwhile, immigrants had withstood several challenges to their legitimacy. The **Immigration Restriction League** had tried many times to require immigrants to pass a literacy test. For their part, immigrants were annoyed that they had to go to school, they hated Prohibition, and they hated the settlement houses into which they were often forced by the government. Black people were one group that would not receive much help during the Progressive era. In 1905, W. E. B. DuBois had spearheaded the Niagara Movement, which led to the formation of the **National Association for the Advancement of Colored People**. In 1911 the **National Urban League** was formed to help black people move into the cities.

Effects on Women and Farmers

During the early part of the 20th century, women aggressively pursued more rights. **Sarah Platt Decker** led the **General Federation of Women's Clubs**, a group that worked hard to improve working conditions for women and children. The **International Ladies' Garment Workers Union** was also popular; it received a great deal of publicity after 146 women died in a fire at the Triangle Shirt factory. **Jane Addams** supported Prohibition, as did the Women's Christian Temperance Union and the Anti-Saloon League. **Carrie A. Nation** became famous for attacking saloons with an ax. For their part, farmers were doing much better in the early years of the 20th century than in years past; those who were still struggling joined with the Progressives.

Social Critics and State Reforms

Eugene V. Debs was a prominent Socialist leader during the Progressive era. The **Industrial Workers of the World**, established in 1905 by "Big Bill" Haywood and known as the "Wobblies," was a radical and militant labor union that appealed to unskilled workers. There were some interesting state and local experiments in this period. In Galveston, Texas, the city switched to a commission system in which the heads of various departments were elected. In Staunton, Virginia, the office of the mayor was done away with in favor of a managing council. **Robert LaFollette's** many reforms in Wisconsin led Roosevelt to refer to this state as the "laboratory of democracy." LaFollette tied the university system, the railroads, and the banks to the state government. Governor Woodrow Wilson of New Jersey planned to use corporate taxes to pay for public education.

National Reforms

The **16th amendment** (1913) allowed for an income tax. The **17th amendment** (1913) provided for the direct election of US senators. The **18th amendment** (1919) prohibited alcohol. The **19th amendment** (1920) gave women the right to vote. In the case of **Muller v. Oregon** (1908), the Supreme Court upheld Oregon's 10-hour workday for women. In **Hammer v. Dagenhart** (1918), the Supreme Court declared the Keating-Owen Act of 1916 was unconstitutional. This act had prohibited interstate shipping of goods made in factories that employed children. The Court declared that the regulation of factories was the concern of the states. In response to this decision, many states passed acts banning child labor. The first **minimum wage** (25¢) was established in Massachusetts in 1912. New York established the first lasting workman's compensation rules in 1910. In 1896, Utah had become the first state to limit the workday, to ten hours.

Summary

It is important to note that Progressivism is not synonymous with Socialism; **Progressives** wanted to change the system, while **Socialists** wanted to destroy it altogether. Progressives believed that the government should regulate all business. Moreover, the Progressives wanted to take government out of the hands of the rich and put it into the hands of the common people. Often,

Progressives had difficulty getting organized. This problem had been the death knell of the Populists; the Progressives were able to succeed in spite of their turmoil because they had great leaders: Roosevelt, Taft, and Wilson. The Progressive philosophy was started by a small minority of liberal intellectuals, including William James and Henry Adams. Among the authors who wrote on Progressive themes were Jacob Riis (*How the Other Half Lives*), Frank Norris (*The Octopus*, on railroad corruption), and Upton Sinclair (*The Jungle*, on corruption in the meatpacking industry).

Theodore Roosevelt's Legacy and the Election of 1908

Theodore Roosevelt, like Andrew Jackson, was truly a public servant. Most of his domestic policies really seemed aimed at improving the lot of the common American. During his administration, Roosevelt greatly enlarged the powers of the president. He created the national parks system and gave the Progressive Movement some respectability. In the 1908 election, Roosevelt chose **William Howard Taft** to become his successor. Roosevelt felt confident that Taft would carry on the mission of the Progressives. Taft ran against William Jennings Bryan of the Democrats, a veteran leader who favored a lower tariff and limited injunctions against strikers. Taft won the election, primarily because of his association with Roosevelt.

Taft Presidency

Foreign Policy of Taft (1909-13)

Roosevelt was succeeded in the White House by **William Howard Taft**, who became known for "**dollar diplomacy**"; the United States would loan money to Latin American countries so that these countries could pay off their European debts. The US would also dabble a bit in Latin American politics, trying to influence the governments for the benefit of American business. The Taft administration also wanted to encourage trade with China and therefore helped prop up some American banking interests there. Taft is also known for his association with the creation of the **World Court**. The US, Britain, and France tried to establish an international judiciary. This idea enraged former president Roosevelt; he preferred settling differences on the battlefield.

Tariffs and the Payne-Aldrich Act

Taft was a very cautious president. His administration saw the deepening of the gradual split between Progressive and Old Guard Republicans. Though Roosevelt had promoted him as a Progressive, Taft slowly began to act more like a member of the **Old Guard**. These tensions came to a head over the tariff in 1909. The Old Guard wanted to keep the tariff as it was, while Progressives fought for reductions. After the House and Senate came up with conflicting tariff bills, Taft was able to engineer a compromise; the **Payne-Aldrich Act of 1909** brought the tariff down to 40.8%. This act also contained a corporate tax and the promise of an income tax in the future.

Split Between Taft and Roosevelt

In the Congressional elections of 1910, the radical Progressives (known as the **insurgents**) were able, with the help of the Democrats, to diminish the power of the Old Guard Republicans in the House. Meanwhile, President Taft drifted closer and closer to the side of the Old Guard. In 1909, Secretary of the Interior **Richard Bollinger** leased national land to corporations, incurring the wrath of forester Gifford Pinchot, who asked for a Senate investigation. Bollinger was forced to resign to take the heat off of Taft. In the Congressional election of 1910, former President Roosevelt announced a mixture of Progressive and Liberal ideas called the **New Nationalism program** and was labeled a Marxist. Then, finally, Taft destroyed a merger between US Steel and Tennessee Coal and Iron that Roosevelt had supported, infuriating the former president.

1912 Election and the Legacy of Taft

At the Republican convention before the election of 1912, the incumbent **Taft** was nominated even though **Theodore Roosevelt** had won most of the primaries. Enraged, Roosevelt left the Republicans and formed the **Progressive (Bull-Moose) party**. Roosevelt ran on his platform of **New Nationalism**: voting rights for women and a ban on child labor were among the initiatives. As an interesting side note, while campaigning in Wisconsin, Roosevelt was shot in the torso during a speech but managed to finish the speech in spite of the injury. Ultimately, the election came down to a contest between Roosevelt and **Woodrow Wilson** of the Democrats. These two candidates had similar views on a number of issues, but while Roosevelt was willing to allow some trusts, Wilson wanted to eliminate trusts across the board. Wilson ended up winning a rather comfortable victory. As the Taft presidency came to a close, most observers saw his greatest accomplishments as the "rule of reason," in which the judiciary was allowed to pick which trusts to bust; the **Mann-Elkins Act**, which brought the telephone and telegraph industries under the control of the federal government; and the creation of the **Department of Labor**.

Wilson Presidency

Tariff Reform and the Federal Reserve Act

Woodrow Wilson appointed **William Jennings Bryant** as his Secretary of State; Bryant became known for his policy of "cooling off," wherein volatile situations would be ignored until all parties had a chance to reconsider their positions. One of Wilson's first major acts as president was to push through the **Underwood-Simmons Tariff of 1913**. This reduces the duty rate to 27% and drastically reduced the tariff on a thousand other items. It also included a slightly greater income tax. Another important economic move was the **Federal Reserve Act of 1913**. This set up a national banking system to be overseen by a Federal Reserve Board. The Federal Reserve system would become the first effective national banking system since the Second Bank of the United States and would be one of the great legacies of Wilson's term. It gave the government a ready means to adjust the amount of currency in circulation.

Effects on Trusts

When Wilson entered office, he declared that there was no such thing as a good trust. With the **Federal Trade Commission Act of 1914**, a bipartisan committee of 5 was created to investigate trusts and issue reports to the government and to the public. The creation of the FTC slowed the growth of monopolies. Peeved by the ineffectiveness of the Sherman Anti-trust Act, Wilson supported the passage of the **Clayton Anti-trust Act of 1914**. This prohibited businesses from selling at reduced prices to favored customers if this price discrimination helped create a monopoly. It also prevented so-called "tying contracts," which forbade a purchaser from buying or selling the products of a competitor. The act also outlawed large interlocking directories; formally allowed the existence of labor unions and farm organizations, as well as strikes and boycotts; and declared that no injunctions could be issued unless property was at stake.

Accomplishments of Wilson's New Freedom Agenda

The **Smith-Lever Act of 1914** brought public education into rural areas. The **Smith-Hughes Act of 1917** allocated money for vocational training and home economics courses. The **Federal Farm Loan Act of 1916** divided the US into 12 agricultural districts and established federal farm loan banks with low interest rates. The **Adamson Act of 1916** asserted that railway workers should be paid for a 10-hour day, though they should only be required to work 8 hours. During Wilson's presidency, **Lewis Brandeis** became the first Jewish member of the Supreme Court. In general, then, Wilson believed in regulating business and improving social welfare. He did not, however, see anything wrong with segregation.

Wilson's Moral Diplomacy

Along with his Secretary of State William Jennings Bryant, Woodrow Wilson promoted the view that nations should treat one another ethically. For instance, the **Panama Canal Tolls Act of 1912** had made it so that the US did not have to pay tolls to use the canal, unlike every other nation; Wilson did away with this measure. Wilson's actions in the **Dominican Republic** were more dubious. The Dominican Republic had been in deep debt early in the 20th century, and the Roosevelt administration had been glad to help in exchange for keeping some troops in the country. When in 1916 the Dominican Republic asked the US to leave, Wilson refused and sent in the Marines. It was only in 1940 that the Dominican Republic was no longer considered a US protectorate. A similar scenario occurred in **Haiti**: the US offered to help the tiny nation, but was unwilling to leave when asked (mainly because of economic interest).

US and Mexican Revolution

Mexicans traditionally resented the US for its seizure of Texas and the Southwest. When the US-friendly leader **Porfirio Diaz** was overthrown in 1910 and eventually replaced by the murderous dictator **Victoriano Huerto**, the US sent weapons to his opponents. Then, in April 1914, two American soldiers of the *USS Tampico* were jailed in Mexico, and the US did not receive an apology upon their release. This angered the US, and they, in turn, seized a German ship that was believed to be unloading war materials to Mexico. The only thing that kept the US out of a more serious conflict was the **ABC Mediation**: Argentina, Brazil, and Chile met and convinced Huerto to retire. Still, **Pancho Villa**, a challenger for control of Mexico, continued to antagonize the US; he killed several Americans and was unsuccessfully pursued by American forces.

World War I

America's Role in the Build-Up to War

There had been relative peace in Europe since the end of the Napoleonic Wars in 1815. Many even felt that the age of great wars was over. In 1910, the US had become involved in the **Pan-American Union**, which was organized to settle differences with diplomacy rather than violence. At the **First Hague Conference** in 1899, 26 nations agreed on the principles of mediation, the humane rules of war, and the creation of a permanent court of arbitration. At the **Second Hague Conference** in 1907, 44 nations reaffirmed the old agreements and declared that the payment of debts could not be forced through war. Unfortunately, there would be no Third Hague Conference; it was canceled due to World War I.

Causes

The rise in **nationalism** at the beginning of the 20th century helped contribute to the possibility of war. There was also some conflict between the **imperialist** (France, Britain, and the US) and the **non-imperialist** (Germany, Italy) nations. Many large nations were seeking economic expansion outside of their own borders, and the competition for foreign markets was intense. There was also a complex system of entangling alliances; many countries were involved in several different alliances at the same time. The spark for World War I, though, was the assassination of **Archduke Franz Ferdinand**, heir to the throne of Austria-Hungary, in April of 1914 by a Serbian nationalist. When Emperor Franz Joseph declared war on Serbia, it set off a chain reaction that involved virtually every nation in Europe.

US Attempts at Neutrality

For a while, the US tried to remain **impartial** in World War I, not least because it was making a great deal of money producing supplies for both sides. Among the general public, there was general support for Britain and France, but many German and Irish immigrants supported the Central powers. There were a small group of American citizens who flew missions for the French, known as the Lafayette Escadrille. Gradually, the US government became angry with both sides, even as it tried to maintain trade with both sides. The British blockade of neutral Scandinavia annoyed the US, as did the German's flouting of the rules of war with their aggressive U-boats. In 1915, the British ship ***Lusitania*** was sunk off the coast of Ireland, killing 128 Americans. This convinced many Americans that neutrality could not be maintained.

Increasing American Involvement

During the early years of WWI, the tide of **nationalism** was rising in the US. Many people felt it would be impossible for America to remain neutral; even Theodore Roosevelt decried conscientious objectors. Nevertheless, many **pacifists** objected to any involvement. William Jennings Bryant resigned as Secretary of State after the sinking of the *Lusitania*, advising the US to stay off of British ships, to stop selling weapons to both sides, and to not side so unthinkingly with the British. At around this time, Roosevelt began recruiting and training men as part of the **Plattsburg Experiment**. Finally, Wilson increased the number of troops in both the Army and the Navy with the **National Defense Act of 1916**. Wilson also set into motion a campaign to build more ships.

Election of 1916 and Entrance into WWI

In the election of 1916, **Wilson** narrowly defeated the Republican Charles Evans Hughes. Wilson ran on a **peace platform**. Soon after, however, diplomatic relations were broken off with the Central powers and submarine warfare began. The American entrance to WWI was accelerated by the "**Zimmermann Note**," in which the German minister to Mexico encouraged that country to attack the United States. In 1917, merchant vessels were ordered by Wilson to arm themselves. Among the reasons the US sided with the Allies was the fact that American business was more deeply connected with these countries than with the Central powers. Also, the US had traditionally had stronger ties with Britain and France.

Wilson's War Agenda

On April 2, 1917, Wilson addressed the nation on the subject of World War I. He declared that the conduct of the German U-boats was "a war against humanity itself," and that, if managed successfully, WWI would be "a war to make the world safe for democracy." Four days later, a **declaration of wa**r was passed. The **Selective Service Act of 1917** registered and drafted millions of American men for military service; about 4.7 million Americans served in the war. The American war effort was mainly paid for with borrowed money, though an increased income tax and the sale of war bonds contributed. Wilson also mobilized American industry; the **War Industries Board**, headed by Bernard Baruch, strove to cut waste and create new industries to aid the war effort. The **National War Labor Board**, headed by ex-President Taft, tried to streamline the labor force to aid the war effort.

Contributions of the American Public and Public Opinion of the War

The **18th amendment** to the Constitution, otherwise known as the **Volstead Act**, outlawed alcohol in 1920. This amendment was purported to conserve food, though it was really an attempt to influence public morality. Through the **Food Administration**, Wilson encouraged people to plant "victory gardens," and to skip meat one day a week. The war was also supported through the **Espionage and Sedition Acts of 1917-8**, which made it illegal to say negative things about the war or to interfere with the sale of war bonds. In **Schenck v. US** (1919), the arrest of the Socialist leader Charles Schenck for criticizing the war was upheld by the Supreme Court, which asserted that First Amendment rights were only exercisable when they did not present a clear and present danger to the nation. In **Abrams v. US** (1919), a Russian immigrant critical of the US actions in Russia was also declared to be a clear and present danger.

Perception of Americans Soldiers

The situation for the Allies was desperate after Russia left the war under the **Brest-Litovsk Treaty of 1917**. The US began to convoy British and French ships in an attempt to prevent U-boat attacks. The American soldiers in Europe were referred to as Doughboys, Yanks, and Devil Dogs. Some of the American heroes in the war were **Alvin York** ("Sergeant York"), who reportedly killed 20 and captured 132; **J.J. Pershing**, who led the American Expeditionary Force; and **Eddie Rickenbacker**, a pilot credited with 22 kills. Americans were praised for their efforts at Cantigny, at Reims, and in the Argonne Forest campaign, where there were over 128,000 American casualties.

Wilson's Fourteen Points Program

Wilson issued his Fourteen Points program supposedly to try to create a quick and lasting peace. Also, however, Wilson hoped to draw the Russians back into the war, to inspire the war-weary Allies, and to demoralize the enemy nations by appealing to the dissenting contingents. Some of the changes called for in the **Fourteen Points** were open diplomacy, freedom of the seas, no tariffs, reduced land artilleries, right of self-determination for all people, temporary international control of colonies (not imperialism), and the creation of the **League of Nations**. Wilson's proposal encouraged the Slavic peoples in Germany and Austria-Hungary to resist the war. Its success in defusing the German war effort allowed Wilson to insist that he would only negotiate with a ruler of the people's choice; **Kaiser Wilhelm** was forced to abdicate the throne.

Armistice of WWI and the Treaty of Versailles

On November 11, 1918, the Germans agreed to an **armistice** provided that Wilson's Fourteen Points be used as a treaty. Overall, between 9 and 10 million people died in the war, including 320,000 Americans. In the **Treaty of Versailles** (1919), the **League of Nations** was created to handle international disputes. A number of new countries, such as Poland and Czechoslovakia, were created by this treaty; also, Germany was disarmed and forced to pay war reparations. Later, the Treaty of Versailles would come to be seen as an uneasy mixture of vengeance and conciliation. It also relied too much on the good faith of the signers. Wilson recognized many problems with the treaty, but he felt the League of Nations would be able to correct them in the future.

US and the League of Nations

The League of Nations had five permanent members: Japan, Britain, Italy, France, and the US. Germany and Russia were not included. The League would have a **General Assembly** and a **Court of International Justice**. It would try to use economic sanctions and, if necessary, force to guarantee the territorial integrity and political independence of every nation. The problems the League developed in practice were many: it was almost impossible to set into motion, because a unanimous vote was required for action; it created a number of artificial and unsuccessful countries (Sudetenland, for example); it had no power to regulate economics; it excluded two major nations (Russia and Germany); and it had no power to force a nation to disarm.

Review Video: WWI Overview
Visit mometrix.com/academy and enter code: 659767

US Response to the Treaty of Versailles and the League of Nations

The US Senate rejected both the Treaty of Versailles and the League of Nations. Republicans, including Henry Cabot Lodge, created the "**Round Robin Manifesto**" guaranteeing that the Treaty would not be approved; some felt that the Republicans were hurt that none of their members had been invited to the table in Versailles. Other politicians were simply angry that the Kaiser had not been killed. Wilson attempted to take the matter of the treaty directly to the American people, but he suffered a stroke in 1919 and both the Treaty and the League were rejected by Congress. Lodge issued the **Lodge Reservations**, a rebuttal to Wilson's Fourteen Points, in which he declared that it was an infringement on Congress' power for Wilson to assert that the US military would be used to protect other nations. In the national climate of isolationism and disillusionment that followed the war, it was perhaps inevitable that the US would never sign the Treaty or join the League.

1920s

Election of 1920 and the Background to the 1920s

The election of 1920 was known as the "solemn referendum." In it, Republican **Warren G. Harding** (who had voted against the League of Nations) defeated Democrat James Cox (who had Franklin Roosevelt as his running mate). Harding's election was in part due to his opposition to the League, but also it was due to his being a radical departure from Wilson. As the 1920s began, Americans felt disillusioned; few people felt that WWI would be the end of war, and massive immigration had left the US scrambling for an identity. There was also hostility lingering from the war: anti-radical, anti-immigration, anti-black, and anti-urban groups had broad followings. The general negativity at the beginning of the decade was not helped by the post-war **recession** and a massive outbreak of **influenza** that killed half a million people.

Immigration and Labor Issues at the Beginning of the 1920s

The radical **International Workers of the World** was defunct by 1920, but many people still feared the influx of new ideas (including communism) and immigrants to the US. Indeed, immigrants became the scapegoat for many of the nation's problems. With the **Immigration Restriction Act of 1921**, only a certain quota of immigrants would be allowed into the country. The **National Origins Act of 1924** restricted immigration even further and stipulated that no Japanese would be allowed into the US. Basically, Americans only wanted Nordics to be able to enter the country. Anti-communist sentiment flared up for the first time during this period; **A. Mitchell Palmer**, the attorney general under Wilson, encouraged citizens to "rouse the Reds."

Race Relations in the Early 1920s

In July 1919, there were violent **race riots** because of competition for jobs; in Chicago, a black swimmer crossed into the wrong area of Lake Michigan, sparking another riot. At around this time, the **KKK** increased in popularity in part because of D.W. Griffith's movie "Birth of a Nation," which depicted the Old South as a paradise led by the Klan. The KKK was led by Hiram Evans and had between 4 and 5 million members; it was anti-black, anti-immigration, anti-Jewish, anti-Catholic, and anti-alcohol. Membership in the Klan declined slightly in the wake of some lynchings and as the economy improved. Nevertheless, many black people sought refuge in the big cities, as part of the **Great Black Migration**. Also, at this time, the **Harlem Renaissance** was reinvigorating black culture; this movement included Langston Hughes, Countee Cullen, Duke Ellington, Paul Robeson, and Louis Armstrong. Many black people subscribed to the beliefs of Marcus Garvey, who thought black people should return to Africa.

Provincialism v. Modernity

At the beginning of the 1920s, the American population was evenly divided between city-dwellers and country-dwellers. While the cities were booming in the post-war period, **farmers** found themselves in economic trouble because of their surpluses. At around this time, many writers, including Ernest Hemingway, F. Scott Fitzgerald, and the members of the **Ashcan School,** sharply criticized the growing materialism of the **urbanites**. In 1920, the "noble experiment" of **Prohibition** began; it was constantly undermined by corrupt government and organized crime, and the government lost the money it had made on the taxation of alcohol. Another incident that brought the differences between Americans into sharp relief was the **Scopes Monkey Trial** in Dayton, Tennessee (1925). In this trial, Clarence Darrow successfully defended a science teacher who had taught the students Darwin's theory of natural selection.

Review Video: 1920's
Visit mometrix.com/academy and enter code: 124996

Harding Presidency

When Warren G. Harding came into office, he promised a "return to normalcy." He almost immediately passed the **Esch-Cummins Act of 1920**, which allowed for virtual trusts in the railroad industry. Harding raised tariffs and was known for having a strong Cabinet, which included **Herbert Hoover** as Secretary of Commerce. Harding's administration was also known for a large number of scandals. It was discovered at one point that Attorney General Harry Daugherty was selling pardons, parole, and liquor; his successor, Jesse Smith, was later found to be doing exactly the same thing. In the **Forbes Scandal**, the head of the Veterans Bureau was found to have embezzled $250 million from the organization. In the **Teapot Dome Scandal**, the Secretary of the Interior was discovered to have sold government oil reserves to private interests. Near the end of his term, Harding had a stroke and was succeeded by **Calvin Coolidge**.

Coolidge Presidency and the Election of 1924

Calvin Coolidge won the election of 1924 by distancing himself from the scandals of the Harding administration. He is famous for saying, "The business of America is business," and his administration embodied that credo. He allowed the return of **trusts** (now known as "mergers"), and he made major efforts to protect American business abroad. When struggling farmers looked to the government for help, Coolidge responded by vetoing the **McNary-Haugan Bill**, which would have established a minimum price for agricultural products. The **Clayton Anti-Trust Act** was totally ignored during the Coolidge presidency.

Election of 1928 and Hoover's Agricultural Program

The election of 1928 pitted **Herbert Hoover** of the Republicans against **Alfred E. Smith** of the Democrats. Hoover, who had served as Secretary of Commerce under Harding, was associated with rural voters, Prohibition, and Protestantism and earned a solid victory over Smith after a dirty campaign. Hoover immediately put into action his "self-help" program for agriculture. With the **Agricultural Marketing Act,** he established cooperatives. He also established the **Federal Farm Board** to loan money to farmers and the Grain and Cotton Stabilization Corporation to buy surpluses. Hoover passed the **Hawley-Smoot Tariff of 1930**, which allowed the president to adjust the tariff at his own discretion; Hoover set it at the highest peacetime rate in American history.

Causes of the Great Depression

The Great Depression was the result of a number of converging factors. For one thing, there was an agricultural depression in the 1920s brought on by tremendous post-war surpluses. The automobile and housing industries both experienced diminished demand in the 20s. One major problem was that wealth was so unevenly distributed: one-third of the nation's wealth was controlled by 5% of the population. There was not much in the way of international trade, in part because of Hoover's high tariff. Overproduction on assembly lines led to factory surpluses and unemployment. Finally, there was persistent unsound speculation in the stock markets. By 1929, many stocks were considered to be overvalued and thus no one was buying them. This caused the catastrophic market crashes of **Black Thursday** and **Black Tuesday** (October 24 and 29, 1929), in which 40% of the market value (about $30 billion) was lost.

Hoover and the Great Depression

Hoover's first strategy for combating the Great Depression was to balance the budget, reduce federal spending, keep the US on the gold standard, and just wait it out. Later, he developed some **work-relief programs**, employing people on public work projects. The **Hoover Dam** was one of those projects. Hoover also created the **Reconstruction Finance Group**, which loaned money directly to state and local governments as well as to railroads and banks. Hoover's aid projects were unprecedented; still, he resisted giving direct aid to the people in the form of welfare. World War I veterans descended on Washington in 1932 when they were told that their pensions would not be paid until 1945. These so-called "**Bonus Marchers**" eventually had to be dispersed with force, leading many citizens to believe that the country was descending into anarchy. The **20th amendment**, known as the anti-Hoover amendment, actually brought the date of the next inauguration forward.

Review Video: Causes of the Great Depression
Visit mometrix.com/academy and enter code: 635912

Franklin Delano Roosevelt and the New Deal

Franklin D. Roosevelt was elected president in the election of 1932. He was determined to preserve the US government and tried to calm the general public with his folksy "**Fireside Chats**." As the governor of New York, Roosevelt had been able to experiment with social welfare programs. He was a pragmatist and a follower of the **Keynesian school of economics** which insisted that the government had to spend money in order to get out of the Depression. Unlike Hoover, then, Roosevelt supported massive government spending and little volunteerism; he wanted the government to regulate agriculture and industry and also for it to take an interest in the daily economic decisions of the people.

In the early days of his term, FDR promoted the **3 Rs**: relief, recovery, and reform. He announced a bank holiday for five days to stop the drain on the cash flow. The **Emergency Banking Act** authorized the **Reconstruction Finance Group** to buy bank stocks in order to finance repair. The **Glass-Steagall Act** made it illegal for banks to loan money to people for the purpose of playing the market and established the **Federal Deposit Insurance Corporation** to protect banks. The **Economy Act** cut $400 million from veterans' payments and $100 million from government salaries. Roosevelt had the gold standard and prohibition repealed. The **Federal Emergency Relief Administration** was established to provide $3 billion in direct relief to people.

The **Civil Works Administration**, headed by Harry Hopkins, was established to give people work. The **Civilian Conservation Corps** was a civilian army that built things such as the Blue Ridge Parkway. Other organizations created to **employ** people were the Public Works Administration, the Works Progress Administration, the Tennessee Valley Authority (responsible for the construction of 21 dams), the National Youth Administration (gave work to high school students), and the Rural Electrification Administration. The **National Industrial Recovery Act** tried to encourage fair competition and create scarcity to drive prices up. It established a minimum wage, a maximum number of weekly hours, and the right of labor to organize. In **Schechter Poultry v. US** (1935), the Supreme Court would rule that the NIRA should have been made up of laws instead of codes, because there were too many loopholes.

As part of his **New Deal program** to help the US recover from the Great Depression, FDR established the **First Agricultural Adjustment Administration**. This agency provided farmers with loans to help them with mortgage payments and paid them not to plant or sell agricultural products. The formation of the **AAA** was economically successful but was one of the least popular measures in the New Deal; it would later be declared unconstitutional in Butler v. US (1936). The **Federal Securities Act** stated that the securities dealers must disclose the prices of stocks and bonds. The **Wagner Act of 1935** made it illegal for employers to have blacklists of unionized workers. The **Federal Housing Administration** was established to provide lower interest rates for people willing to repair or purchase a house. The **US Housing Authority** was created to loan money to state and local governments for the construction of low-cost housing.

Resistance to FDR's New Deal

Father Coughlin was a priest who became famous for his radio broadcasts; he blamed the banks and an "international Jewish conspiracy" for the Depression. **Dr. Francis E. Townsend** was a famous advocate for senior citizens who advocated a national sales tax. **Alf Landon** ran against FDR in the 1936 presidential election and was defeated soundly because of his ties to big business. In the **"Court Packing" controversy** of 1937, FDR tried to overcome Supreme Court resistance to the New Deal by increasing the number of justices on the Court from 9 to 15. This attempt was unsuccessful, but Roosevelt was able to fill Court vacancies with New Deal supporters. A final bit of resistance to the New Deal occurred during the so-called "**Roosevelt Recession**" of 1937-8, in which the economy seemed to be making much less progress than before. Many historians attribute this recession to the fact that New Deal programs were getting much less use in this era.

Life of Black Americans and the Great Depression

In the **Scottsboro (AL) case of 1932**, 9 young black men were accused of raping 2 white women. Although the evidence was scant, all 9 of the men were convicted. In **Powell v. Alabama**, the Supreme Court would rule that the men had not been given a fair trial because they had not had adequate representation. At around this time, the white **Harold Ickes** was the head of the NAACP. He worked hard to get New Deal jobs for black people, Thurgood Marshall among them. **Eleanor Roosevelt** also was an advocate for black people in this period. She came into open conflict with the Daughters of the American Revolution after this group denied Marian Anderson, a black opera singer, the right to sing at Constitution Hall. In general, the New Deal helped many black people obtain leadership positions that otherwise would have been closed to them. The Roosevelt administration was the first to show any real concern for black people, so most black people became life-long Democrats.

Latin American Foreign Policy from 1920 to 1945

The US had tremendous financial investments in **Latin America** and most of the government's policy there was aimed at securing these investments. In 1921, the US paid $21 million to **Colombia**, in part for stealing the land for the Panama Canal and in part to keep them from seizing US oil investments. At this time, the US also had bad relations with **Mexico** until the election of President Calles, a pro-American politician. During the Hoover administration, the US tried to promote "good neighborism" with respect to Mexico and the rest of Latin America. In 1934, the **Platt Amendment** gave Cuba full independence. When Batista came to power, however, the US backed him completely and refused to acknowledge any other elected leaders.

America's Introduction to WWII

After the First World War, the US became obsessed with isolating itself from foreign conflicts. The **Nye Committee** studied the war and determined that it had been fought for financial reasons and could have been avoided. Isolationist parties achieved some popularity during this period, including the **America First Committee**, led by Charles Lindbergh, and **SOS** (Stop Organized Slaughter). The **Neutrality Laws** of 1935-7 declared that the US could not sell weapons to another country in a time of war and that US citizens could not travel on the ships of a nation at war. In 1937, FDR delivered the **Quarantine Speech**, in which he asserted that the Nazi "disease" must be contained. Finally, after conflict in Europe had escalated considerably, FDR declared that the US needed to help Britain and be an "arsenal of democracy in the world." The **Neutrality Act of 1940** made it legal for the US to sell weapons on a cash and carry basis. In August of 1941, FDR and Churchill drew up the **Atlantic Charter**, which vowed to destroy Nazism, protect the right of self-determination, and create a World Peace Organization.

Buildup to the Attack on Pearl Harbor

A number of events had created a stormy relationship between the US and Japan long before the invasion of Pearl Harbor. The US influence over the **Treaty of Portsmouth**, which ended the Russo-Japanese War, created a great deal of tension between the two countries. The Japanese were also antagonized by Theodore Roosevelt's parade of the **Great White Fleet** and by the **National Origins Act of 1924** and the **Segregation Laws**, which kept Japanese from entering and assimilating into the US. America also had a cordial relationship at this time with Japan's longtime rival, China. As the Japanese became more belligerent, the US froze all Japanese assets in America and denied Japan the purchase of any more oil or scrap metal. The Japanese then launched surprise attacks both on the American naval base at **Pearl Harbor** and on the **Philippines**, where they hoped to secure some oil.

US Involvement in WWII Concerning Europe and Africa

After the Japanese attack on Pearl Harbor in 1941, the US declared **war** on Japan, after which Germany declared war on the US. Before going after Japan, however, the US first attacked Germany; this was done because the US underestimated Japan industrially and militarily, and because the US feared Britain was on the verge of defeat. **Operation Overlord**, the Allied invasion of the European continent at Normandy, was led in part by General **Dwight D. Eisenhower**. The American generals Omar Bradley and George Patton took part in the **Allied Operation Torch**, aimed at taking back North Africa. At the **Battle of the Bulge**, in Belgium, the Germans tried to break the Allied lines, but were unsuccessful, in part because of the heroism of American soldiers.

US Involvement in WWII Concerning Asia and the Pacific

The US strategy for controlling the Pacific was known as "island hopping." In the **Coral Sea Battle of 1942**, Americans stopped the Japanese from taking Australia and New Guinea. In the same year, the **Doolittle raids** of Japanese naval bases boosted American morale. In the **Battle of Midway** (1942), the US sunk four Japanese aircraft carriers. In the **Battle of Leyte Gulf**, General Douglas MacArthur took back the Philippines and also took control of Iwo Jima and Okinawa. During this period, a team of American scientists led by Robert Oppenheimer was developing the **atomic bomb** in Los Alamos, New Mexico. Japan was warned several times by President Truman that the bomb would be used if they did not surrender. Surely enough, Americans dropped atomic bombs on **Hiroshima** on August 6, 1945, and on **Nagasaki** three days later. Japanese leaders surrendered aboard the USS Missouri on August 15, 1945.

Election of 1940 and American Home Front During WWII

In 1940, **FDR** easily defeated the Republican Wendell Willkie. After his election, Roosevelt pledged that every resource would be devoted to winning the war. FDR created a number of war-time bureaucracies, including the **War Production Board** (which was devoted to manufacturing goods for war), the **War Manpower Commission** (which organized the draft and created jobs for women), and the **Office of Price Administration**, which set prices and rations. In total, the US war effort cost between $330 and $360 billion. Most of this cost was covered through taxation and the sale of government bonds. The US frequently denied civil liberties to Japanese Americans during this period, forcing many to live in internment camps. In **Korematsu v. US** (1944), the Supreme

Court ruled that the internment camps were legal, but in **ex parte Endo** (1944), the Court adjusted its decision to state that the US could only intern those whose disloyalty could be proven.

Yalta Conference

The Yalta Conference was held on an island in the Crimean Sea in February of 1945. It was attended by FDR, Churchill, and Stalin. At the Conference, FDR tried to make sure that Germany would not be split into smaller nations (this would happen later). Stalin "liberated" the countries along the border of Nazi Germany, and in exchange, FDR allowed the Red Army to remain in those countries. This Conference established boundaries and a provisional government for Poland (this provisional government was led by the Soviets, and would last until 1989). One of the more important moves of this Conference was that the US and Britain allowed a Communist government under **Mao Zedong** to remain in Mongolia; this group of Communists would eventually take over China in 1949.

Truman and the Fair Deal

When Truman came into office after the death of Franklin Roosevelt in 1945, he was already fighting an uphill battle. Many people felt that the Democrats had controlled the executive branch for too long, and many expected **Truman** to have the personal charisma of FDR. Truman gamely attempted to continue the reforms of the New Deal, which he renamed the **Fair Deal**. Nevertheless, he was frequently thwarted by the Republican Congress. Truman surprisingly won a narrow victory over Dewey in the election of 1948, and continued to pursue reforms in education, health care, and civil rights. He gradually became worn down by his conflicts with Congress, however, and he declined to run in 1952.

Korean War

The Korean War took place during the Truman presidency. Korea had been divided after WWII into a **northern half** (under Soviet control) and a **southern half** (under American control). When foreign troops finally withdrew from the peninsula, North Korea attacked South Korea in an attempt to unify. The United Nations Security Council declared that North Korea was an aggressor, and sent troops led by the American General **Douglas MacArthur** to the region. MacArthur had some early victories, but progress slowed when China began to send men and supplies to the North Koreans. Gradually, combat gave way to armistice talks, yet those these too seemed to drag on endlessly.

Election of 1952, Eisenhower, and the Suez Canal

General **Dwight Eisenhower**, a Republican, defeated the Democrat Adlai Stevenson in the election of 1952. One of the first crises of the Eisenhower administration concerned the **Suez Canal** in Egypt. The conflict began after Israel attacked Egypt in response to attacks on the new Jewish nation that were launched at Egyptian bases; at the same time, England and France withdrew plans to build a dam on the Suez Canal because of Egypt's recognition of Communist China. Angered by these events, Egyptian President **Nasser** seized the assets of the European company that administered traffic on the canal. The United States was eventually able to defuse the situation; this marked the introduction of the so-called **Eisenhower Doctrine**, in which American troops and money would be used to undermine Communism in various regions around the world.

Anti-Communism in the United States

As the US was becoming more embroiled in the Cold War, Americans became increasingly paranoid about the spread of **Communism**. There were numerous investigations aimed at weeding Communist spies out of the government, and two people, Julius and Ethel Rosenberg, were executed for spying. The leader of much of this was Senator **Joseph McCarthy**, who was famous for promoting and prolonging the "**Red Scare**" as the often-termed witch-hunt for communists in the government was known (Soviet communications released after the fall of the Soviet Union confirmed the vast majority of his accusations). The tide of anti-communism extended into a general disapproval of organized labor. The **Taft-Hartley Act** restricted the ability of labor unions markedly. In order to survive, the nation's two largest labor unions combined, forming the **AFL-CIO**.

Civil Rights Under Eisenhower

For a long time, the problems of black people had been considered a Southern issue; however, massive black migration into the Northern cities made civil rights a national question. In **Brown v. Board of Education** (1954), the Supreme Court ruled that segregation in public schools is unconstitutional. After some southern states defied this decision, Eisenhower was forced to send in federal troops. At the same time, black people were staging nonviolent protests across the south. **Rosa Parks** famously refused to give up her bus seat in Montgomery, Alabama, and four black men staged a sit-in at a whites-only lunch counter in Greensboro, North Carolina. With the **Civil Rights Acts** of 1957 and 1960, black people were given the right to vote, but these acts were not enforced.

US Foreign Policy Under Eisenhower

The Secretary of State under Eisenhower was **John Foster Dulles**, who wanted to pursue an aggressive foreign policy to "roll back Communism." This was also the period in which the national defense budget skyrocketed, as both the US and USSR believed that peace could be maintained by threatening the other side with total annihilation. It was in this climate that the US first became involved in **Vietnam**. The French had been kicked out of this Southeast Asian nation for good in 1954, and the country had been divided into a northern and southern half in the **Geneva Truce** of the same year. The US then tried to bolster the standing of the non-communist leader **Ngo Dinh Diem** in the south, as he batted the communist **Viet Cong**. Increasingly, Eisenhower was funneling money to the anti-communist forces in South Vietnam, believing that if this country became communist, others would follow (the "Domino effect").

Election of 1960, Kennedy and the Space Program, and Assassination of JFK

In the election of 1960, the Democrat **John F. Kennedy** defeated Richard Nixon; this was the first election in which television was a major factor. One of the most important issues of the Kennedy presidency would be the **space race** with the Soviet Union. It was under Kennedy that the **National Aeronautics and Space Administration** was established. Alan Shepard became the first American in space in 1961, and in 1969, Neil Armstrong would become the first human to walk on the moon. Kennedy, unfortunately, would not witness this event: he was shot and killed by **Lee Harvey Oswald** in Dallas in November of 1963. Though some still claim that Oswald was a part of a broader conspiracy, an investigation led by Chief Justice Earl Warren declared that he had acted alone.

Civil Rights During the Kennedy Years

The black struggle for **civil rights** intensified during the Kennedy administration. After integration at Southern universities was mandated, National Guardsmen were deployed to keep the peace. The situation was especially tense in Alabama, where Governor George Wallace declared that segregation would stand in his state forever. In July of 1963, **Martin Luther King, Jr.** led the famous **March on Washington**, during which he made his "I Have a Dream" speech. King would receive the **Nobel Peace Prize** in 1964. The **23rd and 24th amendments** to the Constitution were aimed at redressing the issue of black suffrage; they gave electoral votes to Washington, DC, and eliminated the poll tax.

LBJ and Election of 1964

Lyndon Baines Johnson took over as president after the assassination of Kennedy. He was able to use the "ghost" of the assassinated president to pass the **Civil Rights Act of 1964**. Johnson also declared a "war on poverty," a system of programs aimed at helping the poor. In the election of 1964, the escalating conflict in Vietnam was much in the public's mind, and the Republican candidate, Barry Goldwater, was viewed as a war-monger. The election of Johnson, however, did not keep the US out of Vietnam. After being elected, Johnson promoted legislation under the banner of the "Great Society." He created Medicare and Medicaid with the **Social Security Act of 1965** and established the agency of **Housing and Urban Development**.

Civil Rights Movement During the Johnson Years

The summer of 1964 saw more violence in the South as three civil rights workers were murdered while trying to register voters. After the passage of the **Voting Rights Act of 1965**, Johnson would have to deploy Federal Marshals to escort black people to the polls. Frustrated by the slow advance to equality, many black people became more militant. During the summer of 1967, there were riots in 150 cities, most of which were sparked by economic concerns, as black people felt they were being mistreated in the marketplace. Advocates of **Black Power** joined groups like the Black Panthers and the Mau Mau, and even formerly moderate groups like the SNCC would begin to endorse violence. Many white Americans who sympathized with the black struggle were alienated by this militancy. There were more riots in 1968 after the assassination of Martin Luther King, Jr. in Memphis. The **Civil Rights Act of 1968** gave full rights to black people but contained restrictions aimed at reducing racial violence.

Foreign Policy Under Johnson

After an American ship came under fire from **North Vietnam** in the Gulf of Tonkin, Johnson received a blank check for American involvement in the region. **General Westmoreland** oversaw troops during this period of escalation. Soon, 184,000 American soldiers were in Vietnam, and the government was spending a million dollars every day. Coupled with inflation, this expense bled Johnson's domestic program dry. The **peace movement** in the US took off during this period. Many people protested what they saw as inequities in the draft system (for instance, black people seemed to be unfairly overrepresented). The US problems in Vietnam were exposed to the world during the **Tet Offensive** of January 1968; during this period, the Viet Cong damaged American forces in virtually every city in the region.

Election of 1968 and Domestic Policy of Nixon

In the election of 1968, the Republican **Richard M. Nixon**, who had narrowly lost to Kennedy in 1960, defeated the Democrat Hubert Humphrey. The **Democratic National Convention** had endured violent protests over the Vietnam War. Though much of Nixon's administration would be concerned with the war (and later with the Watergate investigation), he did institute a somewhat successful policy of sharing revenue with states. The economy was languishing in a state of stagflation (high inflation and high unemployment) during this period and thus Nixon tried to jolt it with a ninety-day wage and price freeze. This move, known as the **New Economic Policy** (or Nixonomics) was a total failure.

Nixon and Vietnam

Nixon had won the election on a platform of "Peace with Honor," and upon entering office, he began slowly withdrawing troops from Vietnam. The **Nixon Doctrine** asserted that the US would honor its commitment to South Vietnam with material rather than men. Nixon did, however, order an invasion of purportedly neutral **Cambodia**, where the Viet Cong were stockpiling weapons. It was also during Nixon's presidency that four students at Kent State University were killed by the National Guard during a protest. In the election of 1972, Nixon crushed George McGovern after Foreign Advisor Henry Kissinger claimed that peace was "at hand." After the election, Kissinger and Le Duc Tho would negotiate the **Paris Peace Accords of 1973**.

Watergate Scandal

On June 17, 1972, a break-in was thwarted at the **Democratic National Committee office** at the Watergate Hotel in Washington, DC. It was eventually discovered that the burglars had ties to the Nixon administration. This began the unraveling of an enormous conspiracy of corruption in the Nixon administration. Many of Nixon's advisers would be forced to resign, though Nixon still refused to cooperate with the investigation. Eventually, though, evidence would mount against him, and Nixon would be forced to release tapes of his Oval Office conversations. Nixon **resigned** on August 8, 1974, although he never admitted any guilt. The **Watergate scandal** left a permanent stain on the presidency.

Gerald Ford Interlude

Gerald Ford, a congressman from Michigan, had been appointed vice president under Nixon after the resignation of Spiro Agnew, and became president after Nixon resigned. His was a mostly uneventful term, as the nation recovered from the shocks of Vietnam and Watergate. Ford talked a great deal about battling inflation but never did very much to back up his rhetoric. It was during the Ford administration that **South Vietnam** fell once and for all to the North Vietnamese. Ford's most famous act may have been his full **pardon** of Nixon. Though Ford at the time declared that "our long national nightmare is over," this unpopular move may have cost him the election in 1976.

Election of 1976 and the Carter Administration

The Democratic governor of Georgia, **Jimmy Carter**, defeated the incumbent Gerald Ford in the election of 1976. Carter was popular with black voters and was generally believed to be outside the cesspool of Washington politics. Carter immediately made an $18 billion tax cut, and inflation soared. Carter also made the controversial move of pardoning all those who evaded the draft during the Vietnam War. "As for foreign policy, Carter became known for his humanitarian efforts, working for peace between Israel and Egypt at Camp David and in 2002 earned the Nobel Peace Prize 'for his decades of untiring effort to find peaceful solutions to international conflicts'" (www.nobelprize.org). Carter signed a bill to give the **Panama Canal** back to the Panamanians, and endured a severe oil shortage. This, along with the failed rescue of fifty American hostages in Iran, led to Carter's defeat in 1980.

Election of 1980 and Foreign Policy Under Reagan

In the election of 1980, known as the **Conservative Revolution**, **Ronald Reagan** easily defeated Jimmy Carter. Reagan presided over the last few years of the Cold War. In 1983, Reagan authorized the invasion of Grenada, where there was an airstrip that was supposedly being used by the Cubans and the Soviet Union. Later in 1983, a Marine barrack in Lebanon was blown up by terrorists, killing hundreds of American soldiers. Reagan introduced the **"Star Wars" program**, a strategic defense initiative in which incoming missiles would be destroyed from outer space by laser-armed satellites. Reagan promoted the "**Peace through strength**" method of foreign policy, whereby the economic might of the United States would furnish such an intimidating military that the Soviet Union would be unable to compete financially and thus fail. This eventually played a major role in the **fall of the Soviet Union** in 1989. Reagan nevertheless improved relations with the Soviet Union diplomatically, even signing a treaty with Soviet Premier **Mikhail Gorbachev** to ban a certain class of nuclear weapon.

Domestic Affairs Under Reagan

Upon entering office, Reagan implemented **tax cuts** in the hopes of stimulating the economy. While this had a very positive effect on the economy by the end of his first term, the American trade deficit continued to grow wider. Reagan's presidency was tarnished by the **Iran-Contra affair**, in which it was determined that the US had sold weapons to a hostile nation. In 1984, due to an impressive economic recovery and unprecedented growth, Reagan defeated Walter Mondale (whose running mate was Geraldine Ferraro, the first female vice-presidential candidate) in a landslide, winning 49 states electorally. In the case **Wallace v. Jaffree** (1985), the Supreme Court ruled that schools could provide for a moment of silence, but could not endorse any particular religion. In **US v. Eichman** (1990), the Court ruled that burning the American flag qualified as expressive conduct, and was therefore permitted under the First Amendment.

Overview of George H. W. Bush's Foreign and Domestic Policies

In the election of 1988, the Republican Vice President **George H.W. Bush** defeated Michael Dukakis easily. Under Bush, the **federal deficit** continued to rise, and the US role in the Iran-Contra affair continued to cast a shadow over the executive branch. One of the major crises during the Bush administration was the wreck of the **Exxon Valdez**, which created the largest oil spill ever along the Alaskan coast. Meanwhile, Bush led the US military into the **Persian Gulf War** in 1990-1 after Iraq invaded neighboring Kuwait. American troops routed the Iraqis. It was also during Bush's administration that the **Berlin Wall** fell and the Communist regime in the Soviet Union finally crumbled.

Election of 1992 and Domestic Policy Under Clinton

The Democratic governor of Arkansas, **Bill Clinton**, defeated the incumbent George H. W. Bush and H. Ross Perot (Independent) in the election of 1992. Clinton tried to reduce the federal deficit. He also pushed for gays to be allowed into the military. Clinton appointed Janet Reno as the first female Attorney General and also reversed most of the restrictions on abortions that had been established by the Reagan and Bush administrations. Clinton's presidency would be plagued by scandals throughout; he and his wife were accused of making illegal land deals in the **Whitewater scandal**, and Clinton would later be **impeached** for lying under oath and obstructing justice in regard to an extramarital affair. A Democrat majority in the Senate elected not to remove him from office.

Election of 1996 and Foreign Policy Under Clinton

In the election of 1996, the incumbent **Bill Clinton** narrowly defeated Kansas Senator Bob Dole. During Clinton's two terms, the United States trade deficit would continue. In the aftermath of the collapse of the Soviet regime, the US gave substantial aid to Russia and many of the new republics. The United States would also supply troops for a **NATO peacekeeping effort** during the Civil War in the former Yugoslavia between the years 1992 and 2000. American troops also participated in peacekeeping missions in Somalia, Bosnia, and Haiti. Finally, Clinton ordered air strikes against Iraq after it was determined that Iraqi leader **Saddam Hussein** had been part of a conspiracy to assassinate President Bush.

Election of 2000 and George W. Bush

In the election of 2000, **George W. Bush**, the son of ex-President Bush, defeated Vice President Al Gore, despite losing to Gore in the popular vote. Bush immediately instituted a major tax cut; critics claimed that this tax cut only benefited the very rich. On September 11, 2001, the US suffered the worst **terrorist attack** in its history, as four planes were hijacked and two of them destroyed the **World Trade Center** towers in New York. The attacks were planned and funded by **al-Qaeda**; an Islamic fundamentalist group led by Osama bin Laden. The United States almost immediately launched **Operation Enduring Freedom**, an attack on the Taliban government of Afghanistan that had harbored bin Laden.

Barack Obama

In 2008, Barack Obama, a senator from Illinois, became the first African American US president. His administration focused on improving the lot of a country suffering from a major recession. His major initiatives included:

- Economic bailout packages
- Improvements in women's rights
- Moves to broaden LGBT rights
- Health care reform legislation
- Reinforcement of the war in Afghanistan

Donald Trump

In 2016, Donald Trump, previously a real estate developer and television personality, was elected 45th president after a tumultuous election in which he won the electoral college but lost the popular vote. Marked by tension between the administration and domestic media, Trump's initiatives included:

- Appointing three Supreme Court Justices: Neil Gorsuch, Brett Kavanaugh, and Amy Coney Barrett
- Passing a major tax reform bill
- Enacting travel and emigration restrictions on eight nations: Iran, Libya, Syria, Yemen, Somalia, Chad, North Korea, and Venezuela
- Recognizing Jerusalem, rather than Tel Aviv, as the capital of Israel
- Responding to the novel coronavirus (SARS-CoV-2) outbreak

Almost completely along party lines, Donald Trump was impeached by the House on charges of abuse of power and obstruction of Congress; he was acquitted by the Senate.

Chapter Quiz

Ready to see how well you retained what you just read? Scan the QR code to go directly to the chapter quiz interface for this study guide. If you're using a computer, simply visit the online resources page at **mometrix.com/resources719/clepushistii** and click the Chapter Quizzes link.

CLEP Practice Test

Want to take this practice test in an online interactive format?
Check out the online resources page, which includes interactive practice questions and much more: **mometrix.com/resources719/clepushistii**

1. What made the election of 1896 different from past elections?

a. It demonstrated that the popular news media need not be engaged in an election campaign.
b. It demonstrated the relative unimportance of financial advantages when running a national campaign.
c. It demonstrated the effectiveness of new campaign tactics
d. It firmly aligned the Republican Party with the interests of free trade
e. It showed that a Democrat could be competitive in the Northeast

2. Which of the following groups would have been disliked by white southerners during reconstruction?

a. Copperheads and Scalawags
b. Carpetbaggers and Copperheads
c. Carpetbaggers and Mugwumps
d. Copperheads and Mugwumps
e. Carpetbaggers and Scalawags

3. During the 1880s, immigrants to the United States came mostly from which pair of nations?

a. Italy and Poland
b. Mexico and Cuba
c. China and Japan
d. Ireland and Germany
e. Sweden and France

4. Consider the 1903 editorial cartoon shown below:

This cartoon depicts Teddy Roosevelt as baby Hercules wrestling snakes with the heads of Senator Nelson Aldrich and J.D. Rockefeller. The snakes represent which corporation that was ordered broken up by the Supreme Court in 1911?

a. U.S. Steel
b. General Electric
c. Northern Securities
d. American Harvester
e. Standard Oil

5. What was the Teapot Dome scandal?

a. A scandal during the election of 1884 in which future president Grover Cleveland was rightfully accused of fathering a son out of wedlock.
b. A scandal during the Grant administration in which government officials diverted tax revenue from the sale of whiskey
c. A scandal during the Harding administration involving oil companies bribing a cabinet official to lease government oil reserves at very favorable rates
d. A scandal during the Grant administration in which government officials received kickbacks from a company that was building the transcontinental railroad
e. A scandal during the Garfield administration in which postal officials were profiting from bidding on the sale of postal routes in the western United States.

6. Which of the following was an effect of the Triangle Shirtwaist Fire?

a. There was a slowing of industrialization because of fear of another disaster
b. Safety equipment was installed to extinguish fires in multistory buildings
c. New labor laws were passed in New York to prevent industrial accidents and protect workers
d. There was increased safety awareness in major American cities
e. There was less regulation of industry in order to stimulate the economy

7. Justice Brown's Majority Opinion:

"We consider the underlying fallacy of the plaintiff's argument to consist in the assumption that the enforced separation of the two races stamps the colored race with a badge of inferiority... If the civil and political rights of both races be equal, one cannot be inferior to the other civilly or politically. If one race be inferior to the other socially, the Constitution of the United States cannot put them upon the same plane."

Justice Harlan's Dissenting Opinion:

"I am of the opinion that the statute ... is inconsistent with the personal liberties of citizens, white and black, in that State, and hostile to both the spirit and the letter of the Constitution of the United States."

The preceding pair of passages comes from which of the following Supreme Court cases?

a. Loving v. Virginia
b. Heart of Atlanta Motel v. United States
c. Brown v. Board of Education
d. Dred Scott v. Sanford
e. Plessy v. Ferguson

8. Prior to writing books like *The Enormous Room*, *Three Soldiers*, and *A Farewell to Arms*, the American authors E. E. Cummings, John Dos Passos, and Ernest Hemingway were inspired by their service as ambulance drivers during which conflict.

a. The Spanish-American War
b. World War I
c. World War II
d. The Spanish Civil War
e. The Russian revolution

9. After its publication, John Steinbeck's the *Grapes of Wrath* became a sensation for its depiction of what group of poverty stricken Americans?

a. Tenant Farmers fleeing Oklahoma during the Dust Bowl
b. Japanese Americans confined to internment camps during World War II
c. African Americans struggling to survive as sharecroppers in Mississippi
d. Hispanic Migrant Fruit pickers in California's Salinas Valley
e. European Immigrant factory workers in Chicago

10. Why was the railroad so important in 19th century America?

a. Railroads were constructed primarily for the military in order to move men and equipment around the country to fight Native Americans and later, Confederates.
b. Railroads were built primarily to force cattle ranchers to start fencing in their herds instead of grazing them on the open range
c. Railroads were constructed as a luxury travel option that happened to became useful to industry eventually.
d. Railroads became a way for dishonest businessmen to confiscate money from the federal government with promises of cheap transcontinental transportation.
e. Railroads provided reliable, year-round transportation to and through areas unreachable by canals, rivers, and wagons.

11. Place the following events of the Progressive Era in the correct chronological order. Place the earliest event first.

I. Pure Food and Drug Act prohibits sale of mislabeled or adulterated products
II. The Grange is founded to help improve agricultural practices and shipping rates
III. The Child Labor Act prohibits the sale of goods produced by children under the age of 14
IV. The Nineteenth Amendment, guaranteeing women's suffrage, is passed

a. I, IV, II, III
b. I, II, III, IV
c. III, II, IV, I
d. II, I, III, IV
e. II, III, IV, I

12. The Norris-Laguardia Act (1932), the Wagner Act (1935), and the Taft-Hartley Act (1947) all concerned the actions of what type of group?

a. Labor Unions
b. Political Parties
c. Civil Rights Advocacy Groups
d. Farmers' Cooperatives
e. Actor Guilds

13. Which of the following best describes John Hay's Open Door Policy?

a. It extended the Monroe Doctrine to China and Japan
b. It declared that every major world power should have equal trading rights in China
c. It established the United States' intention to fight the spread of communism
d. It reversed the provisions of the Chinese Exclusion Act
e. It was a free trade agreement with Mexico and other Central American nations

14. During the first one hundred days of Franklin Roosevelt's presidency, Congress enacted a number of bills that focused on which issues affecting the nation during the Great Depression?

a. Agriculture, Banking, and War in Europe
b. Agriculture, Banking, and Unemployment
c. Banking, Unemployment, and War in Europe
d. Banking, Civil Rights, and Unemployment
e. Civil Rights, Unemployment, and War in Europe

15. The creation of the Tennessee Valley Authority (TVA) in 1933 was intended to do which of the following for parts of Tennessee, Alabama, Mississippi, and Kentucky that were adversely affected by the Great Depression?

a. Raise the educational standards of the region by building new schools
b. Improve the economic prospects for the region by building transportation infrastructure
c. Ensure the conservation of the forest ecosystems in the region
d. Create a series of infrastructure projects to provide the region with cheap electricity
e. Assist local farmers in improving the yield of their land through crop rotation and the use of fertilizer

16. Which of the following events helped lead America into an armed conflict with Spain?

a. The sinking of the *Titanic*
b. The attack on Fort Sumter in Charleston Harbor
c. The sinking of the *Maine*
d. The massacre at the Alamo
e. The sinking of the *Lusitania*

17. Which of the following groups would NOT have been part of a New Deal coalition?

a. White Southerners
b. Minority groups
c. Blue-collar workers
d. White-collar professionals
e. Farmers

18. Mark Twain's *The Adventures of Huckleberry Finn* is an example of which literary movement?

a. Naturalism
b. Transcendentalism
c. Realism
d. Modernism
e. Harlem Renaissance

19. Which of these is NOT a reason that Progressivism grew in the early 20th Century?

a. Anti-monopoly sentiment
b. Concerns over consumer safety
c. Opposition to corrupt political machine politics
d. Growing isolationist sentiments
e. Fear of socialist revolution

20. First proposed in 1870, with proponents such as Charles Sander Peirce, William James, and John Dewey, this mostly American philosophical phenomenon was known as

a. Existentialism
b. Pragmatism
c. Romanticism
d. Common sense realism
e. Logical positivism

21. Which of the following was NOT true of the Presidential Election of 1912?

a. It was the only election between 1896 and 1932 in which a Democrat was elected
b. It was the last election in which a third party candidate finished second
c. It was the first election in which all 48 contiguous states participated
d. It was the last election in which the Socialist Party fielded a presidential candidate
e. It was the last election in which Theodore Roosevelt ran for election

22. The Palmer Raids occurred as a result of which of the following?

a. Anti-German propaganda
b. Southern partisans refusing to accept the end of the Civil War
c. Anti-Communism sentiment (Also known as the Red Scare)
d. The blatant unfairness of Jim Crow laws
e. The United States refusal to ratify the Treaty of Versailles

23. Franklin D. Roosevelt's Good Neighbor policy was meant to

a. provide for the peaceful return of the US-controlled Panama Canal Zone to Panama
b. allow the US to send Lend-Lease aid to Britain and its allies through Canada during the Second World War
c. improve relations with Latin American countries by not interfering in their internal affairs
d. provide affordable housing for the poor during the Great Depression
e. allow the US military to station troops in European controlled Caribbean nations during the Second World War

24. Which of the following best describes the Scottsboro boys?

a. They were a group of African Americans falsely accused of rape and sentenced to death
b. They were civil rights workers killed in Alabama during a voter registration drive
c. They were a group of starving children photographed during the Great Depression
d. They were a World War II African American Army regiment from Alabama
e. They were a group of navy sailors from Alabama who participated in the Zoot Suit Riots in Los Angeles

25. Social Darwinists would agree with which of the following statements?

a. Good citizens ought to help others, especially the less fortunate
b. All men are created equal and endowed by their creator with certain unalienable rights
c. Humans are the sum of their free will choices
d. Warfare between nations is a net positive good
e. Government should provide a strong social safety net

26. Consider the following excerpt from a speech by President Franklin D. Roosevelt:

"This is preeminently the time to speak the truth, the whole truth, frankly and boldly. Nor need we shrink from honestly facing conditions in our country today. This great Nation will endure as it has endured, will revive and will prosper. So, first of all, let me assert my firm belief that the only thing we have to fear is fear itself—nameless, unreasoning, unjustified terror which paralyzes needed efforts to convert retreat into advance."

Which challenge to the American nation is President Roosevelt speaking of in the passage?

a. The bombing of Pearl Harbor by the Japanese
b. The racism faced by African Americans in the South
c. The struggling American economy during the Great Depression
d. The threat of Nazi Germany to the world
e. The political opposition to the New Deal

27. What was the purpose of the 1924 National Origins Act?

a. To restrict immigration from nations outside of Western Europe and Latin America
b. To encourage a greater sense of unity among immigrant communities
c. To encourage more immigrants to come to America
d. To encourage greater diversity throughout the United States
e. To specifically limit immigration from Japan

28. The Great White Fleet was

a. an American battle fleet sent on a promotional trip around the world
b. a Russian battle fleet that fought against the Japanese during the Russo-Japanese War
c. a German battle fleet that blockaded the French coast during World War I
d. a German battle fleet that sank the Lusitania to help bring the United States into World War I
e. an American battle fleet sent to patrol the Panama Canal region and assure its protection

29. Which of the following describes the purpose of the Kellogg-Briand pact?

a. The agreement renounced war as an instrument of national policy
b. The agreement provided a plan for the redevelopment of Germany after World War I
c. The agreement clarified the border between France and Germany after World War I
d. The agreement provided a redevelopment plan for Europe after World War II
e. The agreement allowed European Jews to immigrate to the United States before World War II

30. Place the following events related World War II in the correct chronological order. Place the earliest event first.

I. Japan bombs Pearl Harbor
II. The U.S. declares war on Germany
III. Germany invades Poland
IV. The U.S. declares war on Japan

a. II, I, III, IV
b. III, II, I, IV
c. III, I, IV, II
d. IV, I, III, II
e. III, I, II, IV

31. What is the significance of the Lend-Lease Act?

a. It allowed American soldiers to fight alongside British and French soldiers during World War II
b. It bolstered the National Recovery Administration's efforts to help during the Great Depression
c. It provided favorable terms for immigrants seeking to buy farm land
d. It allowed the United States to provide weapons and supplies to countries fighting against Germany without officially entering World War II
e. It provided financial assistance for farmers during the Great Depression

32. Which of the following best describes why the Chinese Exclusion Act of 1882 was passed?

a. Chinese immigrants were causing overcrowding in Western cities
b. Americans were unhappy that Chinese immigrants were taking jobs in the West
c. Americans found Chinese culture incomprehensible
d. Chinese immigrants refused to enlist in the American Army
e. Chinese immigrants refused to learn English or assimilate into the American culture

33. In the year 1900, 95% of the production generated by the slaughtering/meat-packing industry was clustered geographically

a. in Dallas, Tulsa, and Oklahoma City due to their proximity to large cattle ranches
b. in Chicago, Omaha, and Kansas City due to their status as railroad hubs
c. in New York, Philadelphia, and Boston due to their status as established urban centers
d. in Chicago, Dallas, and New York due to their size and financial power
e. in Baltimore, New Orleans, and New York due to their status as major trade ports

34. Operation Paperclip carried out by the American Office of Strategic Services in the aftermath of World War II was a program to

a. infiltrate the Soviet government
b. shelter refugees from the Holocaust
c. bring German scientists to the United States
d. rebuild Western European economies
e. resettle Japanese-Americans who had been kept in internment camps

35. Why did bimetallism, the policy of allowing a nation's money to be tied to both silver and gold based on fixed exchange rates, grow in popularity among citizens of the Great Plains and West during the late 19th century?

a. The policy would give a financial advantage to locally produced grain over imported grain
b. The policy would lead to lower grain prices
c. The policy would cause inflation, thus raising the price of agricultural products
d. The policy would help mitigate economic inequality
e. The policy would give white farmers an advantage over former slaves who now had their own farms

36. At the time of its annexation, Hawaii was primarily known for the production of what resource?

a. Cotton
b. Sugar
c. Coffee
d. Textiles
e. Fruit

37. Which of the following best describes the League of Nations?

a. It was created by Woodrow Wilson
b. It was a post-WWI alliance of the war's victors, intended to contain Germany and the Soviet Union
c. It was a temporary international commission created to arbitrate territorial disputes
d. It was an intergovernmental organization created after WWI to maintain world peace
e. It was a global free trade agreement

38. What was the primary reason Franklin D. Roosevelt forced more than 100,000 Americans to live in internment camps during World War II?

a. To prevent German-Americans from helping Germany invade the east coast
b. To prevent German-Americans and Italian-Americans from spying on the U.S. government
c. Because of war hysteria and racial prejudice against Japanese-Americans
d. It was a secret government strategy to plant double agents among those spying on the United States
e. Because of fear of another civil war stirred up by Nativists and Isolationists

39. Why would some conservatives oppose the New Deal?

a. The New Deal failed to provide enough support to women, Native Americans, and African Americans
b. The New Deal limited the number of available jobs
c. The New Deal was focused on the domestic economy and took money away from foreign programs
d. The New Deal restricted public ownership in favor of private ownership
e. The New Deal centralized power through the federal government instead of the states

40. Which of the following best describes the reason the United States entered World War I?

a. The sinking of the RMS Lusitania which resulted in the death of 128 Americans
b. The revelation of Germany's attempts to entice Mexico to attack America
c. The U.S. was an ally of Great Britain and France and bound by treaty to enter the war to support the Allied powers
d. The overthrow of the Russian Czar destabilized Eastern Europe and required American intervention
e. The assassination of Archduke Franz Ferdinand destabilized Eastern Europe and required American intervention

41. Henry Ford's views as published in the *Dearborn Independent*, the rise of the KKK in the 1920s, and the speeches of Charles Coughlin in the 1930s, demonstrated the prevalence of which of the following issues in American society?

a. Isolationism
b. Sectionalism
c. Populism
d. Anti-Semitism
e. Anti-Catholicism

42. What was the primary reason for tension between the United States and Great Britain in the 1890s?

a. The borders of Latin America countries
b. The Asian colonies of the British Empire
c. The impressment of American Soldiers by the British Navy
d. The unification of Germany
e. The Boer War in Africa

43. Which of the following was NOT a reason some Senators opposed the Treaty of Versailles?

a. They feared a provision for collective security would lead the US into another war
b. They wished to isolate themselves from international affairs
c. They feared the League of Nations might be too powerful
d. The treaty did not adequately punish Germany for their role in the war
e. They did not wish to cooperate with non-democratic regimes

44. The painting shown below is called *American Gothic* by Grant Wood.

The painting is an example of what school of American art represented by Grant Wood, John Steuart Curry, and Thomas Hart Benton?

a. Impressionism
b. Regionalism
c. Surrealism
d. Expressionism
e. New Deal art

45. What was most significant about the Supreme Court ruling in the 1873 *Slaughterhouse cases*?

a. It justified government power to control commerce for public health benefits
b. It struck down Jim Crow laws as part of Congressional Reconstruction
c. It was the first test and interpretation of the recently passed 14th amendment
d. It was the first government regulation of the Meat Packing industry in the United States
e. It paved the way for more African-American butchers

46. Consider the poem below:

Well, son, I'll tell you:

Life for me ain't been no crystal stair.

It's had tacks in it,

And splinters,

And boards torn up,

And places with no carpet on the floor—

Bare.

But all the time

I'se been a-climbin' on,

And reachin' landin's,

And turnin' corners,

And sometimes goin' in the dark

Where there ain't been no light.

So, boy, don't you turn back.

Don't you set down on the steps.

'Cause you finds it's kinder hard.

Don't you fall now—

For I'se still goin', honey,

I'se still climbin',

And life for me ain't been no crystal stair.

This poem was written by which twentieth century American poet?

a. Robert Frost
b. Walt Whitman
c. Maya Angelou
d. Langston Hughes
e. Emily Dickinson

47. Which of the following is most responsible for the Jim Crow laws (segregating Whites and Blacks) across the south?

a. Plessy v. Ferguson
b. The 14th Amendment
c. Poll taxes and voter literacy tests
d. The end of Reconstruction
e. The KKK

48. Which of the following indicates the winner and the compromise that was reached in order to resolve the disputed Election of 1876?

a. Republican Rutherford Hayes became president and agreed to end Reconstruction
b. Democrat Samuel Tilden became president and agreed to continue Reconstruction
c. Republican Rutherford Hayes became president and agreed to end protectionist tariffs
d. Democrat Samuel Tilden became president and agreed to appoint Republican justices to the Supreme Court
e. Republican Rutherford Hayes became president and agreed to bimetallism

49. Which of the following was NOT a contributing factor to the economic hardships seen in the United States during the Great Depression?

a. Lack of government regulation in American businesses
b. Extreme Income Inequality
c. Overproduction of crops
d. Unemployment rising as a result of new technologies displacing labor
e. Prohibition eliminating tax revenue from the sale of alcohol

50. Tennessee Williams, Eugene O'Neill, and Arthur Miller are all primarily remembered for what type of literary works created during the 1940s and 1950s?

a. Poems
b. Plays
c. Novels
d. Operas
e. Short Stories

51. Mary White Ovington helped found which group below?

a. KKK
b. NAACP
c. ACLU
d. AIM
e. IWW

52. George Washington and Ulysses S. Grant were two-term presidents who arguably could have sought – and won – a third term, but didn't. That precedent that they adhered to was broken by which of the following presidents?

a. Calvin Coolidge
b. Franklin D. Roosevelt
c. William McKinley
d. Woodrow Wilson
e. Warren G. Harding

53. The construction of the Panama Canal was primarily meant to

a. increase economic ties between the US and Latin America
b. divide Panama and Colombia
c. facilitate quicker and safer transits for ships between the Pacific Ocean and the Atlantic Ocean
d. showcase US prowess and expertise in architecture and engineering
e. serve as a basis for the US to project power in the region

54. Which of the following best describes the idea of the "Gospel of Wealth?"

a. The amount of wealth one has reveals the amount of God's blessing
b. One must be wise with wealth and save it, rather than spend it on lavish luxuries
c. If one has earned a lot of money, it is his duty to give as much of it to the Church as possible
d. One should accumulate as much wealth as he or she can so that future generations can receive an inheritance
e. It is the wealthy man's duty to distribute his wealth to the poor for the good of society

55. The difference between the ideologies of Booker T. Washington and W. E. B. Du Bois are best described by which of the following?

a. Washington advocated for an immediate end to segregation, while Du Bois wanted a slow change to Jim Crow laws so that African Americans had time to adjust
b. Washington advocated for equal rights for women, while Du Bois mainly advocated for the rights of African Americans
c. Washington believed that African Americans can only end segregation by themselves, while Du Bois argued that segregation can only end with the help of whites
d. Washington believed that blacks must "prove themselves" in order to gain equal rights, while Du Bois called for an immediate end to segregation
e. Washington argued that African Americans should migrate to Africa, while Du Bois was opposed to African migration

56. The Morrill Act was used to establish which institutions?

a. Federally funded prisons
b. Mental asylums which implemented Dorothea Dix's reforms
c. Agricultural and mechanical universities
d. Telegraph offices, especially in the west
e. Primary schools following Horace Mann's lead to increase literacy rates

57. James Black, Carrie Nation, and Frances Willard are known for which cause listed below?

a. Bimetallism
b. Women's Suffrage
c. Workers' Rights
d. Temperance
e. Isolationism

58. Coxey's Army marched on Washington to demand which of the following?

a. The end of segregation
b. Direct support for World War I veterans
c. Creation of jobs by the government
d. Political accountability and the end of the spoils system
e. Better working conditions in factories

59. The events that led to the Haymarket Square Riot in Chicago in 1884 began with a protest in favor of which of the following?

a. Women's Suffrage
b. Abolition of Slavery
c. Better conditions in food production facilities
d. An eight-hour workday
e. The right to join unions

60. Which term best describes Calvin Coolidge's attitude toward the economy?

a. Socialistic
b. Progressive
c. Pro-regulatory
d. Anti-trust
e. Laissez-faire

61. Which of the following was the reason for the controversy surrounding California's Hetch Hetchy Valley from 1907 to 1914?

a. A scandal over land speculation
b. A protest march against the First World War
c. Environmental concerns over the construction of a dam
d. A protest related to low wages for Hispanic migrant farm workers
e. A miners' strike that was broken by the National Guard

62. What pair of policies associated with leader Mikhail Gorbachev lead to the dissolution of the Soviet Union in 1991? The English translations are "openness" and "restructuring."

a. Glasnot and Pravda
b. Mir and Pravda
c. Glasnot and Mir
d. Mir and Perestroika
e. Glasnot and Perestroika

63. Which of the following groups would have been LEAST likely to vote for President Ronald Reagan?

a. Anti-Communists
b. Liberal "Rockefeller" Republicans
c. Social conservatives
d. Pro-military foreign policy advocates
e. White, working-class Democrats

64. The picture below depicts which pair of 1960s folk singers and anti-war activists?

a. Joan Baez and Bob Dylan
b. Joni Mitchell and Elvis Presley
c. Joan Baez and John Fogerty
d. Joni Mitchell and Bob Dylan
e. Joan Baez and Elvis Presley

65. The passage below is from a June 12, 1987 speech by President Ronald Reagan.

"We welcome change and openness; for we believe that freedom and security go together, that the advance of human liberty can only strengthen the cause of world peace. There is one sign the Soviets can make that would be unmistakable, that would advance dramatically the cause of freedom and peace"

In the lines following this passage, what request does Reagan make of Soviet authorities?

a. To allow their athletes to attend the 1988 Olympic games in Seoul
b. To tear down the wall separating East and West Berlin
c. To begin talks on limiting and eliminating nuclear weapons
d. To join a coalition against the Iraqi invasion of Kuwait
e. To open themselves to more fruitful communications among communist and democratic governments

66. The Pentagon Papers, leaked by Daniel Ellsberg, detailed

a. government efforts to overthrow democratically-elected leftist governments in Latin America
b. government efforts to suppress the Civil Rights Movement
c. a plot by the Nixon Administration to bug the Democratic National Committee
d. lies by the American government about the war in Vietnam
e. government surveillance of American politicians and student activists

67. The following passage is an excerpt from a speech given in 2004 by which politician?

"Hope! Hope in the face of difficulty! Hope in the face of uncertainty! The audacity of hope! In the end, that is God's greatest gift to us, the bedrock of this nation. A belief in things not seen. A belief that there are better days ahead."

a. George W. Bush
b. John Kerry
c. Hillary Clinton
d. Sarah Palin
e. Barack Obama

68. What was the "southern strategy" employed by the Republicans during the 1972 presidential campaign?

a. Focused campaigning in the five southern states won by George Wallace during the 1968 campaign
b. Advocating for issues that were important to Southern farmers
c. Appealing to fearful, pro-segregation, conservative Southern white voters
d. Supporting the reintroduction of literacy tests for voting in the Southern states
e. Pledging to prohibit civil rights protests in the South

69. Place the following developments relating to US attitudes to the communist world and general strategy during the Cold War in the correct chronological order. Place the earliest event first.

I. Thirty-Five Nations sign the Helsinki Accords to improve relations between the East and the West.
II. President Reagan gives his "Evil Empire" speech.
III. President Reagan and Secretary Gorbachev sign the Nuclear Forces Treaty.
IV. The North Atlantic Treaty Organization is formed.

a. IV, I, II, III
b. IV, III, II, I
c. I, II, III, IV
d. IV, I, III, II
e. II, IV, III, I

70. Able Archer 83 and 1995's Black Brant are examples of

a. attempts by foreign powers to assassinate US presidents
b. modern art on display in the National Gallery in Washington, D.C.
c. actions that were misunderstood by the Soviet Union and almost led to nuclear war
d. serious breaches of US cyber security by foreign powers
e. incidents that nearly led to war with North Korea

71. The Mann doctrine was

a. in favor of more communication with the U.S.S.R. to prevent military conflict
b. committed to economic stability over political and economic reform in Latin America
c. in favor of an end to militaristic intervention in South American Countries
d. a corollary to the Truman doctrine
e. concerned with greater focus on domestic issues rather than foreign issues

72. The New Left was most opposed to which of the following?

a. New Deal and Great Society programs
b. Failure of various Communist Regimes
c. Economic policies of the 1950s
d. The War in Vietnam
e. Southern White Conservatism

73. The Marshall Plan did which of the following things?

a. Established an aggressive policy of fighting communism around the world
b. Provided Economic aid to Western Europe after World War II
c. Divided Germany into occupation zones following World War II
d. Cemented the "special relationship" between the U.S. and the U.K.
e. Greatly increased military spending, especially for R&D of new weapons

74. What was the Great Migration?

a. Rural farmers moving to large urban cities
b. Working-class Northerners relocating to the Southwest
c. Southern African Americans moving to Northern cities
d. Urban Whites moving to the suburbs
e. Eastern Europeans immigrating to the United States

75. The passage below is taken from which 1962 advocacy work?

"We stand now where two roads diverge. But unlike the roads in Robert Frost's familiar poem, they are not equally fair. The road we have long been traveling is deceptively easy, a smooth superhighway on which we progress with great speed, but at its end lies disaster."

a. *Unsafe at any Speed* by Ralph Nader
b. *An Inconvenient Truth* by Al Gore
c. *On the Origin of Species* by Charles Darwin
d. *Silent Spring* by Rachel Carson
e. *Affluent Society* by John Kenneth Galbraith

76. Which of the following was NOT a provision of the Patriot Act of 2001?

a. Increased domestic surveillance
b. Creating a detention facility at Guantanamo Bay, Cuba
c. Increased security measures for those entering the United States
d. Prevention of money laundering to fund terrorist activities
e. Funding of counter terrorist efforts in law enforcement

77. Which of these nations is NOT a part of NATO?

a. Turkey
b. Great Britain
c. Greece
d. The United States
e. Sweden

78. Which of the following best explains why parents become more protective of children in the 1960's and 1970's?

a. The AIDS epidemic
b. The threat of a Soviet attack
c. The rise of serial killers like Son of Sam
d. The Hippie Free love, pro-drug movement
e. Increased terrorism abroad

79. What was Woodstock and why was it significant?

a. A free rock concert marking the height of the hippie movement
b. A meeting of Western leaders in upstate New York to discuss Cold War strategy
c. A defense agreement between South Vietnam and the U.S.
d. A government program to cut taxes in order to boost the economy
e. A street in San Francisco known as a significant gathering place for hippies

80. The rioters in Chicago during the 1968 Democratic National Convention were concerned primarily with which of the following issues?

a. Securing Civil Rights for African Americans
b. Ending American involvement in the Vietnam War
c. Fighting poverty among minority populations
d. Increasing Worker Rights and safety in American Manufacturing Industries
e. Increasing Military Spending for the Cold War

81. Al-Qaeda and its affiliates carried out terrorist attacks in all of these cities EXCEPT

a. Washington D.C.
b. Madrid
c. New York City
d. Oklahoma City
e. London

82. Which U.S. president below held the office of vice president and president without a single vote being cast for him?

a. George Washington
b. William Henry Harrison
c. Andrew Johnson
d. Harry S. Truman
e. Gerald R. Ford

83. The term *Detente* refers to

a. The relaxing of tensions between the United States and the Soviet Union
b. The Soviet invasion of Afghanistan resisted by the American backed Mujahedin
c. The process of improving American relations with China during the Nixon Administration
d. The code name for the aerial bombing of Cambodia during the Vietnam War
e. Taking the United States off of the Gold Standard.

84. Which of the following American space programs succeeded in landing a man on the moon?

a. Gemini
b. Mercury
c. Apollo
d. Voyager
e. Mariner

85. The Little Rock Nine were

a. a band which became popular in the 1960s during the British Invasion
b. a group of anti-Vietnam War activists from Arkansas
c. a group of lawyers known for their civil rights work on behalf of African Americans
d. the first African American students to attend the all-white Central High School
e. a group of escaped convicts who terrorized part of Arkansas in the 1930s.

86. Which of the following was one of the first crises of the Cold War?

a. The Berlin Blockade
b. The Gulf of Tonkin incident
c. The Bay of Pigs incident
d. The Cuban Missile Crisis
e. Soviet annexation of Poland

87. Which of the following was the famous campaign slogan from the winner of the 1992 presidential election?

a. "Read my lips. No new taxes."
b. "A giant sucking sound going south."
c. "Ask not what you can do for your country."
d. "Freedom is never more than one generation away from extinction."
e. "It's the economy, stupid."

88. The Stonewall Riots occurred in support of

a. Racial equality
b. Environmentalism
c. Pacifism
d. Women's liberation
e. Gay rights

89. Place the following events of the Civil Rights Movement in the proper order. Place the earliest event first.

I. Montgomery Bus Boycott
II. Dr. King delivers his "I have a dream" speech during the March On Washington
III. Executive Order 9981 abolishes racial segregation in the Armed Forces
IV. Voting Rights Act prohibits racial discrimination in voting

a. III, II, I, IV
b. III, I, IV, II
c. I, III, IV, II
d. III, I, II, IV
e. III, II, IV, I

90. Which of the following Supreme Court Cases overturned state anti-sodomy laws?

a. *Lawrence v. Texas*
b. *Roe v. Wade*
c. *Texas v. Johnson*
d. *Obergefell v. Hodges*
e. *Citizens United v. FEC*

91. President John F. Kennedy sought to improve the lives of American citizens through new initiatives. Which of the following was he unable to enact during his time in office?

a. The Peace Corps
b. Medicare
c. Tax cuts
d. The Clean Air Act
e. The Equal Pay Act

92. NAFTA is an agreement between Canada, the U.S., and Mexico to implement what goal?

a. Fair trade
b. Free trade
c. Dollar diplomacy
d. Combating drug trafficking
e. Combating climate change

93. In 1978 Jimmy Carter brokered the Camp David Accords to promote peace between which two nations?

a. The US and the USSR
b. India and Pakistan
c. Egypt and Israel
d. Iran and Iraq
e. East Timor and Indonesia

94. The New Deal coalition fell apart in the 1960s primarily due to

a. dissatisfaction among minority groups who decided to leave the coalition
b. disagreement between various groups in the coalition over civil rights issues
c. lack of political power due to Republican electoral successes
d. strongly conflicting opinions over economic policy
e. conflict between rural farmers and urban union factory workers

95. Which of the following best explains why President Gerald Ford pardoned Richard Nixon?

a. It was part of the "corrupt bargain" between Nixon and Ford where Nixon would resign so that Ford would be elevated to the Presidency
b. He felt that it was necessary so that the country could put past scandals behind them and move forward
c. Because he was a close, personal friend with Nixon and did it as a favor
d. To maintain support among the moderate "Nixonians" in the Republican Party whose support would be crucial if Ford was to win the upcoming election
e. Because the members of Nixon's cabinet demanded it

96. The U.S.'s backing of UN forces in the Korean War was mainly to

a. prevent a Chinese-backed dictator from controlling the Korean peninsula
b. prevent China or Russia from annexing it
c. uphold the Eisenhower doctrine by backing a democratic, capitalist government
d. uphold the Truman doctrine and prevent the domino effect from taking place
e. satisfy popular demand for a colonial empire

97. Why was the case *Brown v. Board of Education* significant?

a. It opened the door for Government grants and subsidies to provide College Scholarships for African American students
b. It upheld the "separate but equal" decision in *Plessy v. Ferguson*
c. It paved the way for School lunch programs to poor students
d. It opened the door for the teaching of evolution in public schools
e. It overturned the decision in *Plessy v. Ferguson* of "separate but equal"

98. The protesters at universities such as Kent State during the late 60s and early 70s were primarily protesting on behalf of which of the following?

a. The decriminalization of marijuana
b. Environmentalism
c. Civil rights for African Americans
d. An end to the Vietnam War
e. Equal rights for women

99. Strom Thurmond, Harry Byrd, and George Wallace were

a. televangelists from the 1960s
b. congressmen opposed to President Johnson's "Great Society" agenda
c. third-party candidates for President who were proponents of Segregation
d. famous American military leaders during the Vietnam War
e. found guilty in the Watergate scandal

100. Who was the first woman to serve on the Supreme Court?

a. Ruth Bader Ginsburg
b. Sonia Sotomayor
c. Sandra Day O'Connor
d. Elena Kagan
e. Sarah Palin

101. The purpose of the SALT talks was to

a. establish economic ties with the Soviet Union
b. end the Soviet invasion of Afghanistan
c. limit nuclear weapons in both the United States and Soviet Union
d. establish peace between Iran and Iraq
e. end the Vietnam War

102. President Eisenhower's New Look policy was

a. the proposed means of removing wasteful and unnecessary New Deal programs
b. a proposed economic policy designed to prevent recessions and ensure American prosperity
c. aimed at fostering a greater commitment to the civil rights movement in the U.S.
d. a proposal to maintain a large strategic nuclear deterrent in order to redirect spending from a large standing army to other domestic needs
e. a proposal to end the Good Neighbor Policy and pursue more direct involvement in Latin American countries

103. The interconnection and interdependence of world economies as a result of trade is also known as

a. globalization
b. protectionism
c. multilateralism
d. interventionism
e. free trade

104. The Truman doctrine influenced U.S. policy toward all of the following countries EXCEPT

a. Nicaragua
b. Chile
c. Afghanistan
d. Vietnam
e. U.S.S.R.

105. The Supreme Court ruling in the landmark case of *Gideon v. Wainwright* in 1963 established

a. the right of defendants to legal counsel at no cost
b. the right of arrestees to be informed of their rights
c. that public schools could not mandate school prayer
d. the right of citizens to burn American flags as a form of free speech
e. the right of states to allow voluntary euthanasia

106. The elections of 1968, 1980, and 1992 are all examples of

a. close elections
b. elections won by third parties or independent candidates
c. realigning elections
d. elections where the victor won by a landslide
e. elections won by Democrats

107. The "Contract with America" was most associated with which of the following American politicians?

a. Newt Gingrich
b. Bill Clinton
c. Tip O'Neill
d. Dennis Hastert
e. Ross Perot

108. The Nixon Doctrine stated that

a. no Soviet intervention in the Americas would be tolerated
b. the United States would escalate the conflict in Vietnam to gain "Peace with Honor"
c. future anti-Communist wars would be fought without the aid of American troops
d. American military policy would focus on expanding the U.S. nuclear arsenal
e. more troops would be sent to defend South Vietnam

109. The House Un-American Activities Committee was formed to investigate which of the following?

a. The Black Panthers
b. Anti-Vietnam War protesters on college campuses
c. The Hell's Angels
d. The Klu Klux Klan
e. Possible revolutionary Communist or Fascist Citizens and Groups

110. Randy Shilts' 1987 book *And the Band Played On* was about which of the following issues?

a. Unemployment among blue collar workers
b. Institutional discrimination against women in the work force
c. Racism faced by African Americans
d. Poverty in Urban America
e. The AIDS epidemic among homosexual men

111. Who debated Nikita Khrushchev in the Kitchen Debate?

a. Dwight D. Eisenhower
b. Ronald Reagan
c. Richard Nixon
d. John F. Kennedy
e. Harry S. Truman

112. Which of the following best describes the provisions of 1996's Defense of Marriage Act (DOMA)?

a. DOMA defined marriage as the union of one man and one woman and allowed states to refuse to recognize same sex marriages performed in other states.
b. DOMA prevented states from discriminating against same sex married couples and provided tax benefits to same-sex couples.
c. DOMA strengthened the tax benefits for traditionally married couples and allowed states to extend the benefits to same-sex couples in certain circumstances.
d. DOMA stated that all marriages were valid and guaranteed equal tax benefits to all couples.
e. DOMA defined marriage as the union of one man and one woman and prevented states from allowing same sex marriage.

113. Which of the following issues contributed most to the humanitarian crisis caused by Hurricane Katrina?

a. Lack of coordination between local, state, and national government relief agencies
b. Inaccurate weather forecasts did not give citizens enough time to evacuate
c. Environmental hazards caused by the storm
d. Inability to transport thousands of poor residents out of the city before and after the storm
e. Failure to properly maintain the levee system around New Orleans by the Army Corps of Engineers

114. Which of the following events led to the decline in use of nuclear power in the U.S.?

a. The Fukushima Daiichi nuclear disaster in Japan
b. The Chernobyl disaster in Kiev, Ukraine
c. The Atomic bombing of Hiroshima and Nagasaki in Japan
d. The Three Mile Island accident in Pennsylvania
e. The Enrico Fermi unit-1 disaster in Michigan

115. Which of the following was the purpose of the Peace Corps?

a. To create stability in volatile areas around the world
b. To find diplomatic solutions to military conflicts
c. To promote world peace and better understanding between Americans and other countries
d. To protest the Vietnam War and the Cold War
e. To spread the message of the flower children and hippie culture around the world

116. Operation Wetback was a plan to

a. free American prisoners of war in Vietnam
b. assist the Panamanians in their freedom fight against Colombia in exchange for U.S. rights to the Panama Canal
c. forcibly deport Mexican immigrants in the U.S. illegally
d. investigate Soviet spies within the State Department
e. send arms to anti-Communist guerrillas in Latin America

117. The Kyoto Protocol was an agreement to take action on which of the following issues?

a. Trade imbalances
b. Climate change
c. International terrorism
d. World peace
e. Civil rights

118. Lyndon Johnson's campaign ran the "Daisy" television commercial during the 1964 Presidential campaign to promote fear that electing Barry Goldwater would lead to what scenario?

a. Economic recession
b. Environmental disaster
c. Nuclear war
d. Increased racism
e. Higher taxes

119. The energy crisis of the 1970's was caused most directly by which of the following events?

a. An oil embargo against the U.S. for supporting Israel in the Yom Kippur War
b. Global oil refining ability being unable to keep pace with global demand
c. Jimmy Carter's personal failure at diplomacy with Iran
d. The U.S. turning to inefficient and ineffective alternative energy sources
e. Russia and China blocking oil exports to America

120. Which of the following events led to the "War on Terror" campaigns in Iraq and Afghanistan?

a. A wave of terrorist attacks on trains and subways in Western Europe
b. The abduction of Patty Hearst
c. The attacks on the World Trade Center and Pentagon
d. The hijacking of TWA flight 847
e. The bombing of the Alfred P. Murrah federal building in Oklahoma City

Answer Key and Explanations

1. C: The use of new campaign tactics is what made the election of 1896 different from past elections. Prior to 1896 it was considered inappropriate for a presidential candidate to appeal directly to voters. Others were supposed to campaign for their candidate. This could be done through speeches, pamphlets, and editorials in newspapers. William Jennings Bryan was relatively unknown and could not count on others to campaign convincingly for him, plus, he didn't have the financial resources to print pamphlets or place editorials in various newspapers around the country. He decided to appeal to the public directly. Bryan traveled more than 18,000 miles and spoke all across the country giving multiple speeches. He gave 500 speeches in 300 days (and spoke 36 times in one day at one of the stops). He reached more than 5,000,000 people with his message. He was only able to raise $500,000 dollars for his campaign. His opponent, Governor of Ohio, William McKinley was able to raise 3.5 million dollars from big business. McKinley conducted his campaign from his front porch. People were brought to his house from all over the country by train. He held well planned and rehearsed meetings that were then passed on to the press to be printed in newspapers all over the country. Bryan won support from rural farmers, while McKinley attracted the support of big business and urban citizens. Bryan was popular and a good speaker, but was portrayed as a radical, while McKinley was seen as a calm, conservative candidate. McKinley barely won the popular vote, but won by a landslide in the Electoral College.

2. E: Carpetbagger was the name southerners gave to northerners who came south after the Civil War. Some of these northerners came south to help freed slaves transition to their new life. They sincerely wanted to help the south rejoin the union and move forward together. However, some of northerners came south in hopes of cheap land, easy profits, and government grants to line their own pockets. Whether they had good or bad motives, any northerner who came south was called a carpetbagger by southerners. Southerners who cooperated with reconstruction efforts and reconstruction governments were branded "scalawags" by their fellow southerners who were bitter for their loss in the Civil War. Some southerners cooperated with the reconstruction efforts from good motives, but some saw it merely as a way to prosper during a time of economic turmoil. Once again, whether their motives were pure or selfish, any southerner who openly cooperated with the reconstruction governments (especially if they helped the recently freed slaves) was considered a scalawag. Copperheads were northern democrats opposed to the Civil War and demanded immediate peace with the South during the Civil War. Mugwumps were Republicans who supported the Democratic candidate during the election of 1884.

3. A: Most "new immigrants" in the 1880s came from southern and eastern Europe, especially Italy and Poland. Swedish and French immigration came before the 1800s. Irish and German immigrants were more prevalent during the early 1800s and Asian immigrants were prevalent in the mid 1800s. Immigration from Latin America was most prevalent in the 1900s.

4. E: Teddy Roosevelt gained a reputation for his progressive agenda and as a trust buster. Through both vertical and horizontal integration, Standard Oil controlled about 85% of American oil sales by 1904. In 1911 the Supreme Court ruled Standard Oil was an illegal trust under the Sherman Anti-Trust act and was forced to break up into 34 different companies. Most agree that Standard Oil founder J.D. Rockefeller was the richest American ever. Many of the 34 new companies formed from the breakup of Standard oil eventually led to the formation of well known oil companies such as Amoco, Chevron, Exxon, and Mobil.

5. C: The Teapot Dome scandal was a major issue during the administration of President Warren Harding. Secretary of the Interior Albert Fall accepted bribes to help oil companies obtain favorable leases on land containing Navy oil reserves, one of which was at Teapot Dome in Wyoming. Albert Fall became the first Cabinet Secretary in American history to be imprisoned due to his role in the scandal. The other choices all describe other scandals from American History. Grant was troubled by both the Whiskey Ring (B) and the Credit Mobilier Scandal (D). Garfield dealt with the Star Route Scandal (E) and Cleveland won the presidential election despite the controversy regarding his illegitimate son.

6. C: The Triangle Shirtwaist Fire occurred in a New York City garment factory due to unsafe work conditions. A total of 146 workers died in the fire leading to public outcry and the passage of the country's most extensive workplace safety laws by the state of New York. Frances Perkins, the first woman appointed to a cabinet position, came to prominence through her work advocating for reforms following the Triangle Shirtwaist Factory fire. FDR appointed Perkins Secretary of Labor in 1933.

7. E: Though each of the cases listed deals with race issues in the United States, the quotes are from *Plessy v. Ferguson*. In the case, Homer Plessy, who was seven-eighths white, sued after he was arrested for buying a ticket and riding in a "whites only", first class train car. The court ruled against him and established a "separate but equal doctrine" that remained in effect until it was overturned by the 1954 *Brown vs. Board of Education* case.

8. B: A number of notable authors served various roles in the military during World War I. Wartime service influenced the production of a number of great works of literature like the three mentioned in the question. Though the other conflicts listed helped to inspire other great literary works, none were as prolific as those inspired by World War I.

9. A: Steinbeck used notes from a Farm Security Administration worker in California to construct the fictional account of the Joad family who flee Oklahoma during the Great Depression and the Dust Bowl to try to find a better life in California. The family's fortunes do not improve when they finally reach California. Steinbeck was lauded for his passionate portrayal of the depths of poverty faced by some Americans during the Great Depression.

10. E: Railroads could operate in any weather, year-round. Canals and rivers could not be used in the winter when they were frozen solid. Trains also could operate around the clock, safely. They could travel at night without need to stop except to restock coal and water to power the steam engine. Mules and horses needed to rest and could not traverse mountainous areas easily. Trains were faster than canal barges and steamboats. The railroad opened vast areas in the West for farming, commerce, and tourism. They safely and efficiently moved people, produce, and products all around the interior of America, easily connecting areas that were unreachable by ship, barge, or wagon train.

11. D: In 1867, President Andrew Johnson commissioned Oliver Kelly to tour the South and collect data on agricultural conditions; this fact finding mission lead to the founding of the Grange. Congress passed the Pure Food and Drug Act in 1906 during the presidency of Teddy Roosevelt. The Child Labor Act was passed by Congress in 1916. The nineteenth amendment granting women the right to vote was ratified in 1920.

12. A: All of the Acts listed focused on the rights of workers and labor unions. The Norris-LaGuardia Act guaranteed workers the right to full freedom of association in labor unions. Employers could not force employees to sign 'yellow dog' contracts as a requirement for employment. Such contracts told employees that they would be fired if they ever joined a union. It also barred courts from issuing injunctions to prevent boycotts or strikes. The Wagner Act created the National Labor Relations Board which still exists and can require employers to engage in collective bargaining. The Wagner Act greatly strengthened organized labor granting many rights to workers and limiting what businesses could do to curtail unions. The Taft-Hartley Act of 1947 (passed over the veto of President Harry S. Truman) undid some of the provisions of the Wagner act. There was fear at the time of communists infiltrating labor unions and fear of the power that many of the largest labor unions could wield. Labor unions could still be formed and collectively bargain, however, it permitted employees to decline membership in a union if they wished. It also granted courts to step in and end strikes after 80 days if a strike threatened national security. It narrowed the definition of unfair labor practices, restricted the political contributions of unions, and required union officers to swear under oath that they did not have any communist affiliations.

13. B: Russia, Japan, Great Britain, and other European countries all gained tremendous wealth from trade with China. The United States did not want to be left out, so John Hay, President McKinley's secretary of state, asked the other major world powers to adopt the policy of allowing all nations to have equal trading privileges within the open ports China authorized. It helped curtail colonial and imperial intentions by other countries and left sovereignty in the hands of the Chinese, while opening trade for American manufacturers.

14. B: Franklin Roosevelt took office in March 1933 the same month that Hitler seized power in Germany through an Enabling Act. War in Europe would not come until September 1, 1939 with Germany's invasion of Poland. Civil Rights did not become a national issue until after World War II. In the first hundred days of FDR's presidency, Congress passed a series of bills to regulate agricultural jobs (AAA), create new jobs (NIRA) and stabilize public confidence in banks (Emergency Banking Act).

15. D: The Tennessee River Valley was particularly hard hit by the Great Depression. The land was over farmed and not productive. Many of the residents of the area were living in poverty. The idea of Senator George Norris was to build a series of dams and other infrastructure to provide a needed economic boost to the region. By providing cheap electricity to the area (through hydroelectric dams) farmers would be afforded new advantages (better flood control among other benefits). Textile mills could be introduced, providing many with new job opportunities. Eventually the hydroelectric power would be used at the Oak Ridge laboratory which played a pivotal role in the Manhattan Project. Although answers C and E are at least partially correct, they were not the major focus of the TVA.

16. C: On the evening of February 15, 1898 an explosion tore the bottom out of the battleship USS Maine anchored in Havana Harbor. It quickly sank and killed over 2/3rds of the crew. The Maine was anchored in the harbor overseeing U.S. interests in Cuba during a local revolution seeking independence from Spain. Initial investigations concluded that external sabotage (a mine) had led to the Maine's destruction. Several U.S. News papers quickly concluded that the Spanish had done it. This caused the American public to quickly call for war with Spain in reprisal. Later investigation and research has led many to conclude that an internal coal fire caused the onboard magazine containing the shells for the large deck guns to explode. Regardless of the cause, the supposition that the Spanish were behind it, combined with other factors, eventually led America to declare war on Spain.

17. D: The New Deal coalition, and consequently the Democratic Party, were weakest with white-collar professionals. Big business had been Republican since the 1896 election and the demise of the Bourbon Democrats through the presidency of Franklin D. Roosevelt. White southerners, minorities, blue-collar workers, and farmers would have all been helped by programs of the New Deal. White-Collar professionals were the least adversely affected by the Great Depression and hence the least likely to be helped by the programs of the New Deal.

18. C: Realism was a literary movement that was a reaction to literary romanticism. Romanticism placed emphasis on the individual and emotion and sought to set forth an idealistic view of reality. Realism described people and places as they are. It sought to depict life as it actual was down to the way people spoke and the things they believed. The characters in realist novels are ordinary people, living ordinary lives. *The Adventures of Huckleberry Finn* realistically described life and people common to the Mississippi River states, including the hypocrisy, beliefs, trials, and struggles of teachers, clergy, slaves, and slave owners.

19. D: The issue of fairness was central to the progressive movement. Monopolies and political machines which sought to eliminate competition and allow insiders to dominate business and politics were strongly opposed. Businesses which sacrificed consumer safety for profit were targeted. Radical Socialists such as Eugene Debs and Mother Jones frightened many. The progressives, however, were not isolationists. Presidents Theodore Roosevelt and Woodrow Wilson both actively sought to engage the international community in a variety of contexts.

20. B: Rationalism and Empiricism have often been at odds philosophically. Rationalism seeks to base knowledge in the realm of the mind and logical deduction. Empiricism seeks to find facts through close observation and the scientific method. Pragmatism was a 19th century school of philosophy that sought to bring these two viewpoints together or at least end the constant debates and insoluble problems between them. Pragmatism was believed to help end the debates between science and religion by determining truth through experiential outcomes. The proponents of this distinctly American philosophy include Charles Peirce, William James, and John Dewey.

21. D: Infighting among Republicans allowed the Democrats to win the only presidential election they would win between 1896 and 1932. Incumbent president William Howard Taft won the Republican nomination, but former president Theodore Roosevelt ran and finished 2nd representing the Bull Moose party. Though Roosevelt lost, he was planning to run again but supported Charles Evans Hughes in 1916 and died in 1919 before the election of 1920. The last two states of the continental U.S., New Mexico and Arizona, became states in January and February of 1912 respectively. (Non-continental states: Hawaii and Alaska, would not become states until 1959).

22. C: Because of the Bolshevik revolution in Russia, U.S. citizens feared Communism would spread to America and endanger their country and freedoms. This fear led to the "Red scare". Part of this fear was due to the increase in labor strikes and membership in labor unions along with terrorist threats from anarchists mailing bombs to government officials. During the final years of the Wilson administration, attorney general A. Mitchell Palmer and a young Justice Department official named J. Edgar Hoover (the future head of the FBI) organized raids in more than 30 cities and 23 states. They arrested almost 10,000 people, deported 500, and deprived many people of their civil rights merely on the pretext of membership in certain organizations. Many court decisions helped stem the tide by ruling that people could not be arrested merely for their membership in a group that was currently suspect (like anarchists or the communist party). They had to have actually broken the law in order to be arrested. Palmer turned instead to the immigration department in order to arrest people who hadn't done anything wrong, but had come to America from other countries and were deemed dangerous.

23. C: The Good Neighbor policy as practiced by President Franklin D. Roosevelt ended ongoing US military interventions in Nicaragua and Haiti, precluded future such interventions, and decreased US interference in their domestic politics until the onset of the Cold War.

24. A: "The Scottsboro Boys" was the name given to a group of 9 African American teenagers who were falsely accused of rape in Alabama. They became a symbol of the injustices faced by African Americans in the legal system. The testimony of their accusers was inconsistent. Medical testimony indicated no evidence of rape in either woman. The women who accused the young African Americans were likely prostitutes who feared prosecution for crossing state lines to pursue their prostitution (which was a felony at the time). Despite insufficient evidence, eight of the nine members of the group were convicted and sentenced to death. There were numerous appeals and retrials going all the way to the U.S. Supreme Court. The final outcome was that 4 of the original 9 defendants had all charges dropped after being in prison for 6 years through all their trials, retrials, and appeals. The remaining 5 all served various amounts of time in jail. All were eventually pardoned and exonerated (most posthumously). It represents one of the darker moments in post-Civil War southern justice.

25. D: Social Darwinism was a popular 19th century philosophy based loosely on a misunderstanding of Darwin's theory of Natural Selection. It contended that societies, people groups, and cultures act similarly to biological organisms where the "fittest" survive. Therefore struggle is important. The people, cultures, and societies that have the most wealth, the most power, and the strongest military are "fittest" and therefore survive. The weaker groups are made to serve the stronger or else eliminated. Warfare under such a view can be a net positive as it demonstrates who is strongest and helps eliminate the weak.

26. C: President Roosevelt spoke these words during his first inaugural address in 1933. At the time the United States was in the Great Depression which had begun approximately four years earlier in 1929. Roosevelt sought to inspire Americans to get beyond the psychological challenges caused by the economic downturn. He described the crisis as being similar to the nation being at war and asked for increased executive power to institute the measures he believed were necessary to end the economic depression.

27. A: The 1924 National Origins Act restricted immigration from Europe to 2% of the population density in the U.S. from that country as determined by the 1890 census. The year 1890 was deliberately chosen because prior to 1890, immigration to the US had come almost entirely from Western Europe. This was done to appease nativist fears that eastern and southern Europeans were bringing supposedly un-American ideologies like Catholicism, socialism, and anarchism to the United States. The law severely limited the immigration of Africans and banned the immigration of Arabs and Asians. The number was further restricted to no more than 150,000 total immigrants (with the percentages from various countries being determined from the 1890 census). These limits did not apply to immigrants from Latin America. The desire for inexpensive labor to work farms in Texas and California allowed unrestricted immigration from countries south of the U.S.

28. A: The Great White Fleet was the popular designation for the U.S. naval battle fleet that circumnavigated the globe from December of 1907 to February of 1909. The steel hulls of the ships were painted white which led to the nickname above. The fleet consisted of 16 battleships along with other escort vessels in two battle groups. It was meant to demonstrate to the world the growing power of the United States. President Theodore Roosevelt wanted it to be known that America could project military power anywhere in the world to promote and protect its interests. It was designed as a strong message to the world powers as well as a means to build national pride.

29. A: Frank Kellogg, the Secretary of State under Calvin Coolidge, and Aristide Briand, the French foreign minister, arranged the pact as a way to achieve peace among all nations. The agreement's official name, The General Treaty for Renunciation of War as an Instrument of National Policy, describes its terms well. Although almost every country ratified the pact, the agreement was ultimately a failure because there were no guidelines on how to punish those nations who did not follow it.

30. C: Germany invaded Poland on September 1, 1939. Japan made a preemptive strike on the U.S. by bombing Pearl Harbor on December 7, 1941, "a date which will live in infamy." President Franklin D. Roosevelt asked for (and received) a Declaration of War with Japan from Congress in the days following the bombing of Pearl Harbor. Hitler declared war on the U.S. on December 11, 1941, after which the U.S. declared war on Germany and fully entered the conflict.

31. D: The Lend-Lease Act allowed for a program by which the U.S. supplied Great Britain and later the U.S.S.R. with war supplies. While the program did violate existing neutrality laws, it kept the Allies fighting until the U.S. joined the war after Japan bombed Pearl Harbor in 1941.

32. B: Mining was an incredibly profitable industry and many immigrants came from around the world for a chance to make a living. The most numerous of these immigrants were the Chinese, who eventually comprised approximately one third of the total mining workforce. Nativist fears grew because of the increase in immigrant laborers and Congress passed the Chinese Exclusion Act in response.

33. B: Chicago, Omaha, Kansas, and St. Louis were the nation's four largest centers of the meat-packing industry in 1900. They were all railroad hubs and located centrally between the cattle supplying regions in the west and the large markets in the east.

34. C: Operation Paperclip was a plan to secretly bring German scientists, engineers, and technicians (many of whom were members of the Nazi party) to American at the end of World War II. Over 1600 were brought to the U.S. through the plan. It was hoped that these scientists would help increase U.S. rocket and atomic technology in order to have an edge over the Soviet Union. German scientist Wernher von Braun was among those brought into the United States as part of the program. He invented the V-2 rocket for Nazi Germany and provided the U.S. with the Saturn V rocket which was part of the Apollo space program which took American astronauts to the moon.

35. C: Bimetallism would have had little effect on the price of foreign grain or the relative situation of African American farmers. It was hoped that the policy would produce an increase in the prices for agricultural products. Greater monetary supply would lead to inflation and an increase in the price for commodities. This would provide more money to farmers to repay loans. However, it was unpopular with wage workers in cities who would have to pay more for food without an increase to their pay scale.

36. B: Hawaii had become a major source of sugar during the 19th century. A new American tariff was set to cut into the profits of the American sugar plantation owners in Hawaii. In order to protect their economic interests they staged a coup and gained control of the Hawaiian government. This was done in order to petition the U.S. Congress to annex them as an American territory. President Grover Cleveland opposed the annexation because he believed that the coup was immoral and asked that the Hawaiian monarch be restored immediately. The acting Hawaiian government refused. When President McKinley came into office a couple of years later, he led the drive to annex Hawaii as an American territory because of the need for a central pacific naval base born from worries about conflict with Spain (who controlled the Philippines). Those worries would eventually be substantiated through the Spanish-American war. Hawaii eventually became a state at the same time as Alaska in 1959.

37. D: Though Woodrow Wilson greatly promoted the League of Nations in the U.S., he was not its creator. The League was a multi-national effort to prevent future wars through group security. All nations would act together to prevent any one nation from waging a war of aggression. A secondary role for the League was to facilitate the peaceful mediation of territorial disputes. It was well intentioned, but failed in its endeavor as World War II would amply demonstrate.

38. C: With Executive Order #9066, Franklin Roosevelt authorized the secretary of war to set up military zones in the U.S. that could exclude certain people groups. This was used to exclude and relocate over 110,000 Japanese people (of which 2/3rds were U.S. citizens) from the West Coast to internment camps in the American interior. The bombing of Pearl Harbor had led to massive war hysteria and fear that Japan was preparing to invade the American mainland through the West Coast. The West Coast contained many military instillations as well as manufacturing plants turning out military hardware. It was feared that the Japanese living there would sabotage, spy on, and in other ways hamper the U.S. war effort. To assuage these fears, all people of Japanese descent living on the West Coast were stripped of their civil liberties and placed in internment camps for the duration of the war. No similar policy was used against German-Americans or Italian-Americans. In the 1988 Civil Liberties Act, the government of the United States formally apologized to Japanese citizens (or their descendants) for depriving them of their civil liberties through internment and admitted the policy was based on "race prejudice, war hysteria, and a failure of political leadership."

39. E: The New Deal's programs greatly increased the power and authority of the Federal government at the expense of the power of the states. It also increased the size of the Federal government immensely. Conservatives tend to favor smaller government and local or state control instead of centralized Federal power. Conservatives were not comfortable with the increased role of the federal government that was a part of the New Deal.

40. A: The Russian Czar had been deposed several years prior to U.S. entry into the war and therefore cannot be a direct reason for America's entry into the war. The assassination of Archduke Franz Ferdinand drew European nations into war due to treaty obligations; however, the United States was able to remain neutral for the first three years of the war because it did not have any treaty obligations. The sinking of the Lusitania also happened 2 years before America entered the war and therefore could not be seen as the reason that America finally agreed to enter the war. Germany's reinstitution of unrestricted submarine warfare (including neutral American shipping) combined with the revelation of the Zimmerman telegram in 1917, caused America to finally declare war on Germany and enter World War I on the side of the Allies.

41. D: Anti-Semitism increased in the United States through the first half of the twentieth century until the end of World War II. American policies such as limiting Jewish immigration in the years before World War II via the Johnson-Reed Act reflected the growing animosity towards Jews. Ford and Coughlin both believed that there was a Jewish conspiracy to control the world through controlling banks and the monetary systems of the world. News of the Holocaust in Europe and public disagreement with the actions of the Nazi government produced a corresponding decline in anti-Semitic views following the war. Even though anti-Semitism has declined in America, it sadly persists in various pockets of American culture.

42. A: Following the independence of Venezuela in 1840, the British government surveyed and set a border for its British Guiana colony (present day Guyana) at the Schomburgk line. The Venezuelan government disputed the border and after the British claimed the Monroe Doctrine to help its claim, President Grover Cleveland stepped in to facilitate a settlement that was reached by a tribunal in 1899. Venezuela accused the tribunal of impropriety in 1962 and reignited this boundary dispute that has never been resolved.

43. D: The Treaty of Versailles punished Germany harshly, so it was not opposed because of leniency. However, the treaty was opposed for a variety of reasons including fear of another war (A), fear of lack of sovereignty due to a strong League of Nations (C), a desire for isolationism after the war (B), and a desire to avoid cooperating with nations that were not Democratic (E).

44. B: This famous and well known painting by Grant Wood was done in 1930. It is a classic example of Regionalism. The focus of regionalism was rural scenes and small towns in the South or Midwest. It focused on depicting realistic scenes that would have been common to people from that region. It was a response to the Great Depression and came to an end in the 1940s primarily due to World War II. This style gave way to a much more "modern" looking Abstract Expressionism through artist like Jackson Pollock.

45. C: Louisiana passed a law requiring all butchers in and around New Orleans to rent space in one particular location in order to work as a butcher for the city. Prior to this, butchers had worked upstream of the city of New Orleans along the Mississippi River. All of the blood, urine, feces, intestines, and other detritus from butchering animals were cast into the river. This offal contaminated the drinking water and caused multiple outbreaks of cholera in New Orleans that killed thousands. To combat this health risk, the city asked the Louisiana legislature to require all butchers who worked near New Orleans to only work in one designated area. Many butchers filed multiple lawsuits to combat this. The Louisiana courts upheld the state law. Therefore the cases were appealed to the U.S. Supreme Court. The butchers argued that their 14th amendment rights were being violated. They used the "privileges and immunities" clause to say they were deprived of the privilege of performing their work where they pleased. This was the first test of the new Constitutional amendment. The butchers were hoping for a broad interpretation of the 14th amendment to win their case. The court argued a very narrow interpretation of the law stating that the purpose of the 14th amendment was to only secure the basic rights of citizens spelled out in the Constitution and was intended to ensure equal protection under the law for the recently freed slaves. This particular decision has received mixed reviews. Court decisions can set precedent. The broad reading of the 14th amendment of later times helped secure and promote civil rights for minority groups. The narrow reading of the law in 1873 helped protect public health in New Orleans.

46. D: This poem, "Mother to Son," was first published in 1922 by Langston Hughes and reappeared in his 1926 collection, *The Weary Blues*. Hughes is the chief representation of the Harlem Renaissance, an African-American cultural and social movement that blossomed in New York City during the 1920s.

47. D: When reconstruction ended in 1877, the Federal troops stationed in the South to maintain order and ensure the continued freedoms of former slaves, departed. And with their departure went many of the freedoms African Americans had enjoyed since the end of the Civil War. In just a few years white Democrats had swept back into power in state legislatures and systematically began depriving freed slaves of their new found rights. They formalized and instituted "separate but equal" segregation statutes (known colloquially as Jim Crow laws). The narrow rulings by the Supreme Court of the 14th amendment (like in Plessy v. Ferguson) along with poll taxes, literacy tests for voters, and the violent acts of the KKK all worked to strengthen segregation and the "separate but equal" fallacy. These things strengthened and enforced the Jim Crow laws, but it was the end of reconstruction with the departure of Federal troops, closing of Freedmen bureaus, and the return to power of white Democrats that caused the era of Jim Crow. Segregation would not end until the civil rights movement of the mid-20th century.

48. A: The election of 1876 ended with twenty electoral votes unassigned because the election results in those states were disputed. Hayes needed all twenty to become president. The commission that decided the election included eight Republicans and seven Democrats and awarded all twenty to Hayes. In an effort to appease Democratic outrage, Hayes agreed to remove all remaining troops from the South and end Reconstruction.

49. E: President Roosevelt wanted to shorten the Great Depression through various means. The measures of the New Deal sought to address agricultural overproduction (e.g., AAA), lack of business regulation (e.g., FDIC), income inequality (e.g., CCC), and unemployment (e.g., PWA). The loss of tax revenue from the sale of alcohol was not a significant influence for the Great Depression. However, the repeal of prohibition engendered good will from many people and the increased tax revenue did provide some help.

50. B: All three are best known for works produced for the stage. Williams is remembered for *A Streetcar Named Desire* and *The Glass Menagerie.* O'Neill is remembered for *Long Day's Journey into Night* and *The Iceman Cometh*. Arthur Miller is remembered for *The Death of a Salesman* and the *Crucible.*

51. B: Mary White Ovington was born in 1865 and raised by abolitionist parents. After hearing a speech by Booker T. Washington and reading about a terrible race riot in Springfield, Illinois (the birth place of Abraham Lincoln), she got together with other progressives (including W.E.B. DuBois) to co-found the National Association for the Advancement of Colored People (NAACP). One of the goals of the NAACP was to advocate for racial equality and the civil rights of African Americans. They also sought to end the horrible practice of lynching. Crucially, the NAACP's Legal Defense Fund would help hire many of the lawyers that fought Jim Crow laws during the Civil Rights Movement. The Ku Klux Klan (KKK) is a white supremacist group which began during reconstruction. It was largely stamped out during the presidency of Ulysses S. Grant, but was reinvigorated during the 1920s. The American Civil Liberties Union (ACLU) was founded in 1920 and had broader aims than the NAACP. The American Indian Movement (AIM) was a movement for Native American civil rights founded in the 1960s. The International Workers of the World (IWW) was a far left trade union founded in 1905 with the goal of creating one worldwide union for all workers.

52. B: Franklin D. Roosevelt was elected to his third term in 1940, and his fourth (and final, unfinished) term in 1944. The 2 term limit was just a tradition begun with Washington, but later it became law as the 22nd amendment to the constitution (which was ratified after the death of FDR) limited each president to only 2 terms in office. The other answer choices are either presidents who died in office (McKinley and Harding) or two-term presidents who never sought a third term (Coolidge and Wilson).

53. C: Prior to the completion of the Panama Canal, all ships that desired to travel between the Atlantic and Pacific Oceans had to pass around Cape Horn (the southern tip of South America). It was a long and treacherous journey. 2 primary locations had been discussed for a man made canal through Central America in order to shorten the transit time from the Atlantic to the Pacific Ocean. One was Panama (which at the time was a province of Colombia), and the other was Nicaragua. The French started the canal in Panama but were unable to complete it. America encouraged an independence movement in Panama and when they separated from Colombia, America immediately recognized their government and independent nation status and concluded a treaty with the newly formed country for the canal. America was able to complete the canal in about 10 years. America owned and controlled the canal until the 1970s. The canal is one of the most important in the world (along with the Suez Canal in Egypt that speeds travel from Europe to Asia without the need to pass around southern Africa at the Cape of Good Hope).

54. E: Andrew Carnegie, the founder of Carnegie Steel, published a paper titled "Wealth", which argued that the rich should not simply keep money for their own personal use. He believed that society is better off if the rich used their wealth to empower the poor. He believed in high government taxation (especially on the estates of the very wealthy). He favored hard work, modest living, and generous giving. He was opposed to those who lived lavish lives (especially if their wealth was inherited and not earned).

55. D: Both Booker T. Washington and W.E.B DuBois wanted equality and full civil rights for African Americans. However, they had differing philosophies and methods they advocated to achieve that end. Washington believed in working through the current system. He believed that if African Americans would pursue education and work hard, they could overcome much of the fear and prejudice of whites and eventually earn their place as equals. He had the long view in mind. He hoped to win people over and change hearts before a change in the law. To this end he established the Tuskegee Institute to train African American teachers. Many whites, especially in the South, favored Washington's view. DuBois believed that true equality would only come if it was imposed by law and therefore worked to promote such laws. He wanted equality established right away, not slowly earned, if at all. He was not convinced that white prejudice and culture would ever accept African American's as equals unless forced to do so. Only through direct action by the government, through laws that were enforced, would African Americans be truly equal and gain full civil rights. DuBois wrote critically of Washington's view and helped start the NAACP, a legal organization founded to pursue DuBois' agenda of full civil liberties for African Americans. They both wanted a change in the laws and full civil liberties. Washington believed that once hearts and attitudes were changed, then the laws would follow. DuBois believed that once the laws were changed, hearts and attitudes would follow.

56. C: The Morrill Act, or the Land-Grant College Act of 1862, was legislation that gave Federal land to states in order for them to sell it and raise money to start state universities with the express purpose of teaching agricultural and mechanical arts (without neglecting other areas of classical study, e.g. liberal arts). The intent of the act was to encourage the education of farmers and engineers through the establishment of A&M universities.

57. D: James Black was the founder and first presidential candidate for the Prohibition Party. Frances Willard was the president of the Women's Christian Temperance Union (WCTU). Carrie Nation is remembered for attacking alcohol-serving establishments with a hatchet in the period before Prohibition.

58. C: The Depression of 1893 resulted in massive layoffs, including about a third of all factory workers. An Ohio Populist, Jacob S. Coxey, proposed that the government employ people to repair roads and other public works projects. Unemployed workers and supporters marched on Washington D.C. 400 began the march and grew to over 500 by the time the march ended. It began in Ohio and finished in Washington, D.C. The march was popular but no changes came because of it. In fact, Coxey and others were eventually arrested for trespassing on Federal property at the end of the march. Even though the movement failed, it did highlight the strong feelings of discontent among workers regarding massive unemployment.

59. D: Women's suffrage would not come until 1919 and slavery was abolished in 1865. The move towards better conditions in factories was a central concern in the early 1900s and the 1935 Wagner Act granted workers the right to join unions. However, the direct precursor to the Haymarket Square Riot was a peaceful protest calling for an 8 hour workday. What began as a protest in favor of an eight-hour workday turned deadly when someone threw a bomb at police who were trying to disburse the peaceful crowd. It is uncertain who threw the bomb, but anarchists were blamed. The riot has been called the most monumental event in the history of labor.

60. E: Republican Calvin Coolidge became president in 1923 following the death of Warren Harding. Coolidge favored small-government and detested regulation of business. Coolidge's administration along with congress lowered taxes to the point that by 1927 only the wealthiest 2% of Americans paid federal taxes. Some historians have argued that Coolidge's laissez-faire policies set the stage for the Great Depression.

61. C: In the aftermath of the San Francisco earthquake of 1906, the city was looking for a water supply that might help mitigate the damage of any future catastrophic event. San Francisco asked the Department of the Interior for and was granted the rights to develop the Tuolumne River in the Hetch Hetchy Valley within Yosemite National Park. John Muir and the Sierra Club were against the development based on concerns that the development would destroy the natural environment. In 1923 the O'Shaughnessy Dam was completed and the Hetch Hetchy Valley was flooded. It provides water and hydroelectric power to the greater San Francisco Bay Area to this day.

62. E: Glasnost and Perestroika were policies of reform implemented by Mikhail Gorbachev in the USSR in the mid-1980s. The new policies granted new freedoms and allowed people to openly criticize the Soviet Government. These new policies opened doors to negotiation with the West which brought an end to the Cold War, and opened the way for freedom and independence for Soviet Bloc countries.

63. B: Ronald Reagan was able to build a strong coalition drawn primarily from White, blue collar, socially conservative voters. Liberal Republicans would not have many of the same goals and political ideals as Ronald Reagan. However, the majority of Americans favored his conservative, strong, anti-communist views.

64. A: Joan Baez and Bob Dylan were both folk music artists. They sang and toured together during the 1960s. They both sang about and advocated against the war in Vietnam. Joan was much more political than Dylan. Joan also participated in and sang about Civil Rights for African Americans. She met Martin Luther King Jr. and helped lead marches for Civil Rights. She advocated for Amnesty International, Freedom of Speech, fair wages for migrant farmers in California, and opposed capital punishment. They sang many songs that helped define a generation and give voice to the turbulent era of the 1960s.

65. B: On June 12th, 1987, President Ronald Reagan gave the speech from which the lines in the question are quoted. He spoke in front of the Brandenburg Gate separating West Berlin from East Berlin. He called on the leader of the Soviet Union, Mikhail Gorbachev, to grant true freedom to all. Reagan called on Gorbachev to open the gate and tear down the wall. The Berlin Wall came down 2 years later in 1989, reuniting Germany and ending Soviet control. There is debate as to how much impact the speech itself had on opening the gate, tearing down the wall, and reuniting Germany, however it is noteworthy as another step in the process that ended the cold war and improved relations between American and Russia.

66. D: The pentagon Papers detailed the history of U.S. involvement in Vietnam starting with President Truman. Truman gave direct military support (money and weapons) to the French in their war against the Viet Minh. The U.S. involvement in Vietnam continued into Eisenhower's presidency, Kennedy's presidency, Johnson's presidency, and Nixon's presidency. It also revealed that America was directly involved in attacking North Vietnam (instead of just protecting South Vietnam), bombing and attacking Laos, and other things not revealed to the American public. These papers were leaked to the press. A brief court battle ensued in an attempt to suppress the information. The Supreme Court in a 6-3 decision said that the first amendment freedom of the press was more important that national security in this case. Other attempts were made to discredit the person who leaked the information. All of the information was finally declassified and made available 40 years after the initial leak. It helped galvanize anti-war groups and led to widespread disillusionment with the government among average Americans.

67. E: In 2004 then Illinois state senator Barack Obama was chosen to give the keynote address at the Democratic National Convention. Obama called his speech "The Audacity of Hope" and later adapted the themes from the speech into a 2006 best seller with the same title. Obama's rising popularity helped catapult him first to a U.S. Senate seat in 2005 and then to the American presidency in 2008.

68. C: Richard Nixon ran for president as the "law and order" candidate. He promised to crack-down on the protests and race riots that were being led by those opposed to the Vietnam War and in favor of African American civil rights. This message resonated with white, middle class, southern, conservative voters who had traditionally voted Democrat. They turned to the Republican candidate because the Democratic Party had, over the last decade, instituted most of the changes they had witnessed across the nation. The Nixon campaign believed correctly that inciting racial tensions in the south would help bring white voters to their side. They played on racial stereotypes and fears to garner political support. In 2005 the head of the Republican National Committee apologized to the NAACP for using polarizing race-based strategies to win elections.

69. A: NATO was founded in 1949, and represented an effort by the United States to contain the spread of communism. The Helsinki Accords were signed in 1975 and represented "detente" or the relaxation of tensions between the east and the west. Reagan gave his "Evil Empire" speech to the British House of Commons in 1982, which indicated a shift towards the rollback of communism. The INF Treaty, signed by President Reagan and General Secretary Gorbachev in December of 1988, eliminated over 2,500 short- and intermediate-range ballistic missiles of both the nuclear and conventional varieties, which gave hope for the coming end of the Cold War.

70. C: Able Archer 83 was a military exercise conducted by NATO in 1983 to test the ability of the various members of the alliance to function during a nuclear exchange with the Soviet Union. Word of the exercise reached Soviet intelligence services, who believed that the exercise was actually a ruse for a real war. The Black Brant scare was an incident where a Norwegian-American group of scientists launched a scientific rocket into orbit to study the aurora borealis. To Russian radar operators, the speed and flight trajectory of the missile resembled that of a submarine-launched ballistic missile. During the incident, Russia's "nuclear briefcase" was activated and presented to Russian President Boris Yeltsin. Both incidents are some of the closest that the world has come to full scale nuclear war outside of the Cuban missile crisis in October of 1962.

71. B: The Mann doctrine (named for American diplomat Thomas Mann), emphasized a pragmatic approach to U.S. relations with Central and South American countries. It maintained that economic stability (which favored American Business interests) in Latin America was more important than promoting freedom and democracy. Therefore, a country that installed a right wing military dictatorship would be supported by America as long as its markets were open to American Business. There would be no opposition to that government even though it was totalitarian. The Mann doctrine was hard line against communist governments and called for intervention and overthrow of such governments. However, the application of the Mann doctrine was ineffective because U.S. government officials couldn't always tell the difference between South American governments that were communist and South American governments that were merely anti-American.

72. D: The New Left arose in America as part of the Youth Movement of the late 1950s and early 1960s. There was great dissatisfaction with the economic models of classic Marxism and labor movements which failed to achieve significant goals. The modest gains of the old liberals were seen as sell outs to corporate greed. The young generation at college during this time did not like the world they were set to inherit. They believed that instead of economic class struggle focused on workers there should be greater emphasis on wealth redistribution, social equality, Civil rights, and free speech. They believed the future belonged to young intellectuals not the workers of the world. They were absolutely opposed to the war in Vietnam and saw it as another sign of American Imperialism. They were in favor of direct action through protests, sit-ins, and demonstrations. Some even went on to form groups in favor of violent protest. This led to bombings by groups like the Weather Underground.

73. B: The Marshall Plan (formally known as the European Recovery Program) was a plan of economic aid to Europe. Specifically, the U.S. gave money to rebuild the infrastructure of European countries devastated by World War II. It was feared that poverty, dislocation, and unemployment would lead European countries to elect communist governments. It was hoped that economic stimulus and rebuilding would help the people but also demonstrate the superiority of democratic capitalism to the peoples of Europe. The Soviet Union and Eastern Bloc countries refused the help, but Western European countries accepted the help with resounding success. Most Western European countries saw economic increases of 15 to 25 percent during the time the plan was in effect. Along with the direct monetary stimulus, the U.S. agreed to provide the military protection Western Europe needed so that they would not have to spend money on defense. They could instead invest that money in infrastructure and economic growth.

74. C: Prior to 1910 over 90 percent of African Americans lived in rural areas in the South. From about 1916 to 1960 more than 6 million African Americans left rural areas in the South and moved to urban areas in the North and West. Many of them were escaping Jim Crow laws, segregation, prejudice, and racism. Many were also looking for better economic opportunities in the rapidly industrializing North. Historians have called it the greatest voluntary migration (not having to move because of war, starvation, or forced relocation) of any people group in the shortest amount of time. By the end of the great migration almost 50 percent of African Americans had relocated to Northern and Western industrial areas from rural Southern areas.

75. D: Rachel Carson wrote *Silent Spring* in 1962. It detailed the adverse effects of massive pesticide use. The widespread use of pesticides (as opposed to targeted and carefully measured application) was leading to the death of birds and other animals that the pesticides were not meant to affect. Also, some of the pests were building up immunity to the pesticides because of its overuse, thus negating the positive benefits in a relatively short amount of time. She sounded an alarm by using science and research and helped start the environmental movement in the U.S. Some have criticized here work and 50 years later there is still a debate revolving around the use of DDT for mosquito control. Her contribution helped raise awareness of manmade chemicals and the possible unintended consequences that could harm both people and the environment.

76. B: The USA PATRIOT Act (Uniting and Strengthening America by Providing Appropriate Tools Required to Intercept and Obstruct Terrorism) was signed into law in 2001 by President George W. Bush as a response to the terrorist attacks against targets in the U.S. on September 11, 2001. This Act empowered the government to collect data through various forms of surveillance from U.S. citizens in order to find terrorists and thwart their plans. Many felt this was a violation of civil rights (like the right to privacy and 4th amendment rights of being secure in our "persons, houses, papers, and effects, against unreasonable searches and seizures"). The Act allowed for greater security measures for those entering the United States, enhanced surveillance techniques, prevention of money laundering in order to fund terrorist activities, and provided funding for more personnel and training for counter terrorism agencies. While many purported terrorists were detained at the facility in Guantanamo Bay, the founding of that detention center was not part of the Patriot act. The detention center was formed by the administration of President George W. Bush under executive order. The formation and maintenance of this detention facility has been the source of much debate and controversy.

77. E: NATO (or North Atlantic Treaty Organization) also known as the North Atlantic Alliance, is a military alliance of 29 different North American and European countries. It was founded in 1949 and is committed to joint military defense. It was part of the cold war and was meant as a buffer to threatened Soviet and Communist aggression. However, Sweden has never been a part of NATO.

78. C: In the seventies, many serial killers became widely known, including Son of Sam in New York City, the Zodiac Killer in northern California, and Charles Manson. These events made parents more concerned for their children's safety. This change has led in part to modern parents constantly monitoring their younger children.

79. A: Woodstock was a music festival held in August of 1969 in New York. It was supposed to last only 3 days, but ended up lasting 7. It took place on a 600 acre dairy farm near White Lake in the town of Bethel (which is near the town of Woodstock, New York). 32 different musical groups performed for 400,000 people who attended. It marked a pivotal moment in music history and the hippy counterculture movement. It was billed as "3 days of peace and music."

80. B: 1968 was a very tumultuous year in America. The assassinations of Robert Kennedy and Martin Luther King Jr. and violent riots in over 100 U.S. cities had the whole country reeling. Many wanted a return to stability and heavily emphasized Law and Order. Others wanted to see things change and felt that only through ongoing large group protests would their voice be heard and heeded. A failure to end the war in Vietnam led many young protestors to gather in Chicago during the Democratic National Convention. The Democratic Party was deeply divided and many of the most popular candidates were seen as maintaining Lyndon Johnson's policy of continuing the war in Vietnam. Because of the unpopularity of the war and a growing movement to end American involvement, these young demonstrators gathered to register their dissent. The Mayor of Chicago called in over 23,000 police, army, and national guardsmen to break up the protests. No permits were granted to those wishing to lawfully gather to protest, but that didn't stop the protesters. 10,000 protesters gathered to let their voices be heard. The ensuing violence was witnessed both inside the convention hall and outside in the streets as police violently attacked and arrested hundreds of protesters. It was a shocking scene to the American public and to the world.

81. D: All of the cities listed have experienced terrorism. On April 19, 1995, the Alfred P. Murrah Federal Building in Oklahoma City was severely damaged by a bomb in a truck parked in front of the building. 168 people died (including children in the daycare on the second floor). Over 680 suffered injuries. The attack was the work of two American terrorists, Timothy McVeigh and Terry Nichols. The two terrorists claimed that they were responding to government actions at the Branch

Davidian compound outside of Waco, Tx, and Ruby Ridge outside of Naples, Idaho. Al-Qaeda claimed responsibility for the other terrorist attacks. Washington, D.C. and New York City were attacked on September 11, 2001. Madrid, Spain suffered bomb attacks on several trains in 2004. London subways were the target of Al-Qaeda sponsored terrorist bombings on July 7, 2005.

82. E: Gerald Ford was appointed Vice President by President Richard Nixon in 1973 when vice president Spiro Agnew resigned due to a scandal in which he pleaded no contest. The following year President Nixon resigned due to the Watergate Scandal elevating Ford to the presidency. He is the only person to reach the White House without a single vote being cast for him as either vice president or president. President Ford immediately pardoned President Nixon as one of his first decisions upon entering office. It was not a popular decision and hurt his chances for being elected in 1976.

83. A: The word Détente means "relaxation." It is used in American history to refer to the easing of tensions ("thawing out" or "un-freezing" of relations) with the Soviet Union between 1967 and 1979. It was a bright spot during the Cold War when there was increased trade between the U.S. and the U.S.S.R., mutual cooperation, and the signing of significant nuclear arms limitation agreements (SALT: Strategic Arms Limitation Talks). This began under the Nixon administration and continued during the Ford administration. The Soviet invasion of Afghanistan saw relations chill between the two countries with a resumption of the Cold War until the time Reagan and the era of Glasnost and Perestroika which Gorbachev helped foster.

84. C: Project Mercury was the first American spaceflight program. It began in 1958 and concluded in 1963. In all, the Mercury program had 6 successful manned launches. Alan Shepard was the first American in space (though Russian Yuri Gagarin was the first human in space). The Mercury program was replaced by the Gemini program (1961-1966). There were 10 successful Gemini manned launches. The goal of Gemini was to perfect the space travel techniques necessary to land a person on the moon (working outside the spacecraft, orbital maneuvers, space rendezvous docking, etc.). All Gemini missions involved a two person crew (unlike Mercury, which had only single person missions). The Apollo program had the goal of landing a human being on the moon. It operated from 1961-1972 and had its first manned flight in 1968. In all, Apollo had 6 successful moon landings (Apollo 13 did not land on the moon because of the explosion of an oxygen tank while on the way to the moon). The first manned moon landing was Apollo 11 (Neil Armstrong, Michael Collins, and Buzz Aldrin). The Voyager program sent two robotic probes through and beyond our outer solar system to study various planets and moons (both Voyager I and Voyager II launched in 1977). The Mariner program sent robotic probes to land on and investigate Mars, Venus, and Mercury from 1962-1973.

85. D: The Supreme Court Case *Brown v. Board of Education* ruled that the segregation of public schools was unconstitutional. The Supreme Court also directed that public schools had to be integrated as soon as possible. The Little Rock school board came up with a plan to gradually integrate its public schools starting with Central High School in the fall of 1957. Nine African American students were chosen, based on their grades and character, to be the first to attend the all-white school. The pro-segregation Governor of Arkansas (Orval Faubus) sent National Guard troops to block the 9 African American students from entering the school. Angry mobs of parents and students protested the 9 students. One female of the Little Rock 9 was even spat on by an older white woman. President Dwight Eisenhower sent troops from the 101st airborne (stationed nearby) to escort and protect the students while at the school. The African American students were subjected to harassment, bullying, beatings, and verbal abuse. One of the 9 students was a senior and went on to graduate with the class of 1958. The governor closed all the public high schools for the 1958-1959 school year as a way to prevent integration. The schools were reopened and integrated the following school year. All 9 were awarded Congressional Gold Medals by President Bill Clinton.

86. A: The Soviets kept portions of Eastern Poland at the end of World War II as part of the territorial concessions agreed upon by the Allied powers. Poland was compensated with German lands in the west. The Bay of Pigs was a failed, U.S. backed, attack by anti-Castro rebels in 1961. The Cuban Missile Crisis involved spy planes flying over Cuba and finding Russian Nuclear Missiles being deployed in 1962. President Kennedy ordered a blockade of Cuba until the missiles were removed. The world came very close to nuclear war during that crisis, but disaster was averted. The Gulf of Tonkin incident (1964) involved an attack on a U.S. Destroyer off the coast of North Vietnam by torpedo boats. It brought the U.S. more directly into the war in Vietnam. The Berlin Blockade was one of the first crises of the Cold War. In 1948 Germany was divided into East and West Germany. Russia controlled East Germany, while the allied powers (France, U.S., and U.K.) controlled West Germany. The Capital of Germany was located in the City of Berlin which was deep in East Germany. The Capital city was also divided into East Berlin (Soviet controlled) and West Berlin (Allied Control). The Russians wanted control over all of Berlin and so they blocked all road, rail, and canal access from West Germany to Berlin. The Allies responded with a massive air supply campaign (called the Berlin Airlift). From June of 1948 until September of 1949, the allies flew a massive number of daily flights to keep the people of West Berlin supplied with food, fuel, and other necessary supplies. Tensions were high and it was feared that there might be open warfare between the Russians and the Allies. However, the Soviets relented and the roads and other transportation options were reopened between West Germany and West Berlin. The wall separating East and West Berlin was finally brought down and Germany was reunited in November of 1989.

87. E: The 1st quote came from incumbent George H.W. Bush. After he was elected in 1988, he signed a bill that included a tax increase. Because he had promised no new taxes it appeared that he had broken his campaign promise. It was strongly used against him in the 1992 election. The 2nd quote is from Ross Perot who was referring to manufacturing jobs going to Mexico instead of staying in the U.S. He ran an amazing campaign for a 3rd party candidate who had never held public office, but in the end could not garner more than 20 million votes and no Electoral College votes. The 3rd quote comes from President John F. Kennedy who called on his fellow citizens to ask what they could do for their country. He was urging them to serve instead of be served, to give instead of take. He was assassinated in 1963. The 4th quote is from Ronald Reagan who was president from 1980 until 1988. The correct answer is E and was a primary slogan of Bill Clinton's campaign. The economy was not doing well in the early 1990s. Bill Clinton's campaign focused on the way he planned to help improve the economy, he also focused his campaign on "Change vs. more of the same", and "Don't forget health care." Clinton only won 43 percent of the popular vote, but got 370 electoral votes (100 more than he needed to be elected). This slogan has been used many times with different endings to emphasize what is important for different people (e.g. It's the deficit, stupid; it's the math, stupid; it's the voters, stupid; etc.).

88. E: At 3 A.M. on June 28, 1969, New York City Police raided the Stonewall Inn, a bar in Greenwich Village. It was known to be a place where Homosexual men and women, as well as transgender peoples could gather safely with like-minded people. The police raided the bar on a semi-regular basis and cited them for selling alcohol without a license and sending everyone home. At the time of the riot it was illegal to cross dress (you had to be wearing at least three pieces of gender appropriate apparel to avoid breaking the law), to solicit homosexual acts, and to dance with someone of the same sex. The police were particularly harsh in this raid and when a lesbian woman was hit over the head with a police baton as she was forced into a van for arrest, she called on others to do something. Prior to this, the crowd at the bar usually quietly dispersed and went their separate ways. However, on this occasion, the crowd remained and when called upon to act, decided to protest. There were about 400 people present and only a handful of police. The crowd began to yell and throw bottles and rocks at the police. The police quickly took cover in the bar while the protesters rioted outside. They attempted to set the bar on fire, but back-up arrived in time to extinguish the blaze and break up the riot. People continued to gather for the next 5 days as the protest spread into the surrounding streets. It was a strong impetus for the growing Gay Rights movement in the U.S. The Stonewall Inn is now a historical monument.

89. D: President Truman signed Executive Order 8802 in 1948 ending segregation in the military. Rosa Parks was arrested for refusing to give her bus seat to a white man on December 1, 1955. It sparked the Montgomery Bus Boycott of 1955-1956. Dr. Martin Luther King Jr. gave his speech during the 1963 March on Washington, a massive political rally demanding civil and economic rights for African Americans. President Lyndon Johnson signed the 1965 Voting Rights Act to guarantee 14th and 15th amendment rights for all Americans, particularly in southern states.

90. A: Prior to 1960 every state had anti-sodomy laws (sodomy being defined legally as deviate sexual practices). Many of these laws were amended to permit heterosexual practice of certain sex acts, while maintaining that same-sex practice of these same sex acts constituted a crime. In September of 1998 John Lawrence was arrested in Northeast Harris County, just outside of Houston, Tx. He was charged with engaging in same-sex practices deemed to be unlawful sodomy by the State of Texas (a class C misdemeanor). It was turned into a test case for anti-sodomy laws. It was argued that forbidding same sex practice of things deemed allowable by heterosexual couples was against the equal protection clause of the 14th amendment. It was further argued that the Supreme Court had found a "right to privacy" in the minority, dissenting opinion of the Bowers v. Hardwick case and that adult, consensual, sexual activity in a private residence could not be criminalized. In a 6-3 decision, the Supreme Court concurred and anti-sodomy laws were struck down in the U.S. *Roe* established the right to abortion, *Johnson* the right to burn the American flag, *Obergefell* the right to same-sex marriage, and *Citizens United* the right to unlimited political expenditures by corporations.

91. B: President John F. Kennedy created the Peace Corps on March 1, 1961 by executive order (#10924) and Congress added their authorization on September 21 of the same year. The Peace Corps' mission was to send volunteers around the world to share knowledge and skills to needy areas of the world. It was hoped that these volunteers would help build bridges to other cultures, share American knowledge and culture, win hearts and minds, promote peace, and help prevent struggling countries from turning to communism. President Kennedy advocated for and asked Congress to pass sweeping tax cuts for rich and poor citizens alike, as well as for corporations. These tax cuts were implemented by Congress at Kennedy's request, in 1963. Kennedy also sponsored legislation meant to control air pollution. The result was the Clean Air Act of 1963. Kennedy also sponsored legislation regarding the pay inequality between women and men. Congress responded favorably by passing the Equal Pay Act of 1963. It addressed the pay discrepancy in companies where women would be paid less to perform the same or similar jobs as men. During the law's first ten years after being signed by President Kennedy, 171,000 employees received back pay totally about 84 million dollars. Kennedy also proposed medical insurance for the elderly in 1963 (it would eventually be called Medicare). However, Congress was unwilling to enact this legislation. It would await the administration of President Lyndon Johnson before it would be signed into law in 1965. Though many of the legislative initiatives undertaken by President Kennedy were implemented, Medicare was one of the few that were not.

92. B: NAFTA is the North American Free Trade Agreement, implemented in 1994 by Bill Clinton. It agreed to add Mexico to a previously existing free trade agreement between Canada and the U.S. In particular, it lowered trade barriers such as protective tariffs in order to encourage the free flow of products and free trade between the 3 countries.

93. C: The Camp David Accords of 1978 were between Israel and Egypt, who had previously fought each other in the Six Day War and the Yom Kippur War. The agreement brought peace between Israel and Egypt. At that time, Egypt was the strongest Arab power in the region. The agreement strained Egypt's relationship with other Arab nations, but prevented further wars involving Israel and Egypt.

94. B: The most important factor leading to the New Deal coalition's collapse was the conflict between the Northern and Southern wings of the Democratic Party over the issue of civil rights. Southern whites were supporters of the Democratic Party and some of them were in favor of the New Deal. However, they were all staunchly against the civil rights movement.

95. B: Gerald Ford's primary motive in pardoning Nixon was to allow the country to move on from various scandals, including the Watergate scandal. The country at the time was suffering from fatigue from politically and racially motivated riots in multiple cities, war burnout over Vietnam, multiple political scandals, and other long drawn out issues. Ford hoped to bring a speedy end to the Watergate scandal so that healing could begin. Many people were angry at Ford for pardoning Nixon and believed that some corrupt political bargain had been struck (but that was not true). It would ultimately cost Ford any chances of being elected during the next presidential election.

96. D: The Truman doctrine stated that the U.S. would send economic and/or military aid to any country to prevent the spread of communism. The belief was that if one country fell to communism, then all the surrounding countries would too, creating a domino effect. This theory was used to justify the Vietnam War. The Korean War ended in a stalemate. The Korean peninsula was divided into two parts separated by a demilitarized zone. There was a communist regime in the North backed by China and a democratic government backed by the U.S. in the South.

97. E: The Supreme Court decision in *Brown v. Board of Education* was really a ruling involving four different cases (of which *Brown v. Board of Education* was the first one listed) involving the "separate but equal" segregation policy that *Plessy v. Ferguson* had enshrined. Separate had been a reality for many decades, but equal had never really been achieved. Courts had ordered many school districts to upgrade and increase funding for African American schools. However, in these cases it was argued successfully that separate accommodations were inherently unequal. The person that was segregated was automatically made to feel inferior and unequal because of the segregation. This sense of being unequal because of being segregated had a negative effect on the thinking of African Americans. It continued to create a strong sense of inferiority in the thinking of young African Americans particularly. The solution would be true equal treatment under the law and educating children together. Desegregation would hopefully end rampant racism and help restore proper equality and brotherhood among American Citizens regardless of the color of their skin. This landmark decision reversed *Plessy v. Ferguson* and helped undo the harm it had introduced with the "separate but equal" fallacy.

98. D: The 1960s and early 1970s saw lots of demonstrations on college campuses and elsewhere. It was a time when many young people wanted their voices to be heard. Students protested for equal rights for women, civil rights for African Americans, environmentalism, and other issues. However, the primary issue that students and others protested was the continued American involvement in the War in Vietnam. Just prior to the Kent State protests and student shootings,

President Nixon had announced that American troops were crossing the border into Cambodia to fight Viet Cong soldiers who were using it as a staging point for incursions into South Vietnam. Anti war sentiment was very strong in the country at the time and there was a strong desire to end hostilities and return American Soldiers home. Ending the war in Vietnam was by far the most important issue that motivated student protests of the era.

99. C: Each man listed ran for president (or was written in) as third party candidates during different elections. Strom Thurmond ran during the 1948 presidential campaign as the States' Rights Democratic Party candidate. He was opposed to Civil Rights Legislation that would end segregation and open voting to African Americans by ending Jim Crow Laws in the South. He received almost 1.2 million votes and garnered 39 Electoral College votes. Harry Byrd was a write in candidate and received 15 Electoral College votes in the 1960 presidential election. Byrd was a strong proponent of segregation. George Wallace ran as the American Independent Party candidate in the 1968 election. He received almost 10 million popular votes and 45 Electoral College votes. He carried the states of Alabama, Arkansas, Georgia, Louisiana, and Mississippi. He is famous (or infamous) for the slogan: "Segregation now… Segregation tomorrow… Segregation forever!"

100. C: Sarah Palin was Governor of Alaska from 2006 to 2009, but was never appointed to the Supreme Court. The other women listed either are now, or have been, Supreme Court Justices. Sandra Day O'Connor, the first woman to be appointed to the Supreme Court, was nominated by President Ronald Reagan. Ruth Bader Ginsburg was nominated by President Bill Clinton, and Sonia Sotomayor and Elena Kagan were nominated by President Barack Obama.

101. C: Shortly after the end of World War 2 the U.S. and U.S.S.R. began an arms race. Part of that race involved maintaining similar numbers of long range nuclear missiles so that one side or the other never felt that an attack would be in their best interest. However, pursuing this strategy merely led to larger and larger arsenals and the stockpiling of greater and greater numbers of world ending Nuclear Missiles. Beginning with the administration of President Lyndon Johnson, the governments of both countries decided it would be in their mutual interest to talk about limiting their nuclear arsenals. These mutual discussions between cold war enemies were called the Strategic Arms Limitation Talks (SALT). They involved finding ways to reduce the size and amount of nuclear armaments and yet maintain equality. The talks lasted over many years (beginning in 1969 and ending in 1979). SALT I and SALT II were the positive results from these talks helping reduce the tension between the two countries as well as limit and reduce the size of their respective nuclear arsenals. The talks came to a halt with the Soviet invasion of Afghanistan in 1979. Further talks have ensued over the years, many with favorable results.

102. D: After World War II the Allied powers pursued a policy of "containment" towards communism and the Soviet Union. This was pursued positively by seeking to rebuild areas devastated by the war and in the third world in hopes of showing how successful capitalism was and help prevent communist governments from coming to power in Western Europe and around the world. Containment was also pursued by maintaining large standing armies, navies, air forces, and pursuing technological advances in armaments and nuclear weapons as a deterrent to possible Soviet or Communist aggression. Maintaining large standing military forces and being able to transport them or maintain bases all around the world was very expensive. Eisenhower wanted to find a strong deterrent, but also find the most cost effective way to maintain containment. The New Look strategy was designed to invest more money in building up nuclear weapons arsenals (both long range ballistic missiles as well as strategic nuclear weapons delivered by long range bombers). It was hoped that through the threat of a massive nuclear retaliatory strike, the Soviet Union would be prevented from taking aggressive military actions around the world. Because the cost of doing this was less than maintaining bases, navies, air forces, and standing armies, the cost savings could be invested in other sectors of the U.S. economy and infrastructure.

103. A: Globalization has to do with the increasing interdependence of peoples and nations of the world through trade, financial investment, advanced technology, and communication. As barriers to world trade are lowered, and greater international financial investment takes place, there is greater interchange and interaction between cultures and peoples. Increased ability to communicate internationally through technological advances such as cell phones and the internet has increased global interconnectedness. There has been increased mobility and ability for people to travel for business and pleasure. The early Asian trade routes (i.e. The Silk Road etc.) allowed different cultures to interact. That has been multiplied many times over through the massive proliferation of modern transportation (air travel, huge cargo ships, massive trucking), technology (computers and the internet), and modes of communication (cell phones). There has been much good that has come from this with many more people being raised above the poverty threshold (defined by the U.N. as people who make less than $1.25 per day). But there have been negative costs associated with all of the increases in trade, transportation, communication, and technology. The environment has suffered from deforestation as well as greater pollution. Technology and advanced communication have been used to coordinate and spread violence around the world through terrorism. All of the increased communication has not necessarily led to greater understanding or decreased violence in the world. Globalization is a fact and in many ways (as with many different things) a mixed blessing.

104. E: In 1947, shortly after the end of World War II, the U.K. asked the U.S. to take over financial support for Greece. Prior to this time the U.K. had given direct aid to Greece. Unable to sustain continued economic aid to Greece, they appealed to America to provide the help. The reason for this had to do with the Greek civil war between the government and communist rebels. It was feared that Greece (and potentially Turkey) would both fall to Communism and grant the Soviet Union unprecedented presence in the region with direct access to Mediterranean ports. President Truman gave a speech to Congress where he spelled out the dangers of rising world communism and fear of Soviet aggression and the peril that America would face if Greece and Turkey both fell under Soviet control. Congress approved 400 million dollars in financial aid, though they sent no troops. Truman's warning about growing world communism led to what has become known as the Truman Doctrine. It stated that America would provide financial and sometimes military support to governments that were threatened by communism. Sometimes this has led America to support rightwing military dictatorships in Central and South American merely on the pretense that they weren't communist. The Truman doctrine was used to justify money, support, and even covert operations to provide aid to the Contras who were fighting the communist Sandinistas in Nicaragua. America used the Truman doctrine to justify removing Chilean leader Salvador Allende in favor of military dictator Augusto Pinochet. It was used again to support sending aid to the Mujahideen in Afghanistan to oppose the Soviet invasion there. And it was part of the rationale for American support to South Vietnam against the North Vietnamese and Viet Minh rebels. Since it was opposed to Soviet aggression and the spread of communism, the Truman doctrine would never provide aid to the U.S.S.R.

105. A: In 1961 Clarence Earl Gideon, an impoverished man, was charged and convicted of petty larceny in Florida. At the time of his trial, he was unable to pay for the services of a defense attorney. He requested that the state provide him with an attorney per the 6th amendment to the Constitution. The court refused stating that they were only required to provide counsel for serious offenses that might result in the death penalty. From jail, Clarence appealed his case with a hand written note that asserted that his 6th amendment rights had been violated. The Florida Supreme Court upheld the lower court ruling, whereupon Clarence appealed to the Supreme Court of the

United States. The Supreme Court, in a unanimous decision, ruled that his rights under the 6th amendment had indeed been violated. He was granted a new trial with legal counsel provided and he was acquitted. The ruling in *Gideon v. Wainwright* established that state courts must provide legal counsel (i.e. an attorney) for defendants who cannot afford one.

106. C: All three of the elections listed are considered realigning elections in that they resulted in the formation of new political coalitions (1980, 1992) or the destruction of an old coalition (1968). A is true of the 1968 election, while D is true of the 1980 and 1992 elections, and E is also true of the 1992 election.

107. A: Newt Gingrich and Dick Armey worked together to outline multiple goals for the House of Representatives if the Republicans were able to win a majority during the election of 1994. This "Contract with America" (derisively called the "Contract <u>on</u> America" by Bill Clinton) was brought out 6 weeks prior to the midterm elections during President Bill Clinton's first term in office. It was popular with conservative middle class Americans. The Republicans did gain a majority in the House of Representatives and worked to bring to a vote all of the various things they had promised in the original document. Some of the things promised in the "Contract" were term limits for Senators and Representatives, Welfare reform, Tax cuts, a balanced budget amendment, an anti-crime bill, and tort reform. Some of the items were indeed signed into law while others were voted down in the Senate or vetoed by President Bill Clinton.

108. C: Nixon wanted to change the focus of how America was involved in supporting its allies militarily. The traditional role of America sending troops was a continued significant drain on the economy. Nixon said in a speech given in Guam that American would honor all of its treaty commitments and extend its Nuclear Deterrent Umbrella over the allied nations that requested it. Furthermore, Nixon stated that America would be willing to supply weapons, and military hardware, along with monetary aid to its allies. However, America wanted its allied friends to shoulder the burden of manpower for these conflicts. America would not be sending troops to these places, but leaving the burden for fighting for their country's freedom to those living there. This doctrine was followed with a few exceptions until the destabilization of the Middle East during the Carter Administration.

109. E: After World War I and the Bolshevik revolution in Russia, Americans became increasingly worried about subversive and revolutionary movements coming into the U.S. through propaganda and immigration. A congressional committee (the Overman Committee) was formed in 1919 to investigate Bolshevik propaganda and groups in the U.S. during the initial "Red Scare". This committee was followed by the Fish Committee (named after Congressman Hamilton Fish III) in 1930. The Fish committee was formed to investigate communist activity in the United States. It was followed by the McCormack-Dickstein Committee in 1934. This committee broadened the scope of investigation to include Nazi propaganda entering the U.S. along with German Fascist sympathizers. In May of 1938 the House Un-American Activities Committee was formed from the former Fish Committee and McCormack-Dickstein Committee. It was charged to investigate alleged subversive or disloyal activity to the America government by individuals, groups, and public employees who might have ties to communist or fascist ideals. Senator Joseph McCarthy set up a similar committee in the Senate but it was separate from the HUAC in the House of Representatives. HUAC used brutal tactics to force people to implicate others and regularly charged individuals who refused to cooperate, with contempt of Congress and incarcerated them. Many Hollywood actors and directors were implicated and "black listed" (they were under suspicion and therefore were not hired for movies and other roles). One of the most prominent cases involved Alger Hiss who was convicted of perjury and sentenced to 44 months in prison. The committee became increasingly unpopular during the 1960s and was finally disbanded in 1975.

110. E: HIV and AIDS probably made their way to the U.S. from Africa through Haiti in the 1960s. But because of the disease's long incubation period the results were not seen until the late 1970s. It finally came to national attention beginning in the 1980s. However, for many different reasons, the national response through the CDC (Centers for Disease Control) and state health services was very, very slow. It seemed people were indifferent and those who were involved seemed to care more for their legacy than merely helping those who were suffering and dying. There were exceptions, but the majority of people in government and in the wider public were not very interested in helping cure a disease that was perceived to be happening almost exclusively to homosexual men. San Francisco Chronicle journalist Randy Shilts wanted to help change that and bring to light what seemed to be criminal indifference to a growing epidemic. He used his skills as an investigative journalist to systematically detail the lack of response from the Federal government, to state health organizations in New York and California, down to city government and individual citizens. It was acclaimed for its unflinching look at something that the American public of the time was not very interested in discussing or acting upon. "And the Band Played On" is a reference to "Business as usual", in other words, no response or change.

111. C: In 1959 Vice-President Richard Nixon travelled to Russia to meet Soviet Premier Nikita Khrushchev at the American National Exhibition in Moscow. Both countries set up exhibits in the other country to showcase their respective cultures and economic accomplishments. As Nixon was showing Khrushchev around the exhibit (which included a full size American home full of modern labor saving devices like a dishwashing machine, and conveniences like televisions), they stopped in the kitchen for an informal, impromptu discussion of the relative merits of capitalism and communism. The good natured exchange became somewhat heated, but ended on a positive note when both leaders spoke of the need for more openness between the two superpowers. Nixon's participation and his comments which were aired on national television increased his popularity with the American public.

112. A: The Defense of Marriage Act was passed by huge, veto proof, majorities in both the House and Senate. President Bill Clinton signed it into law on September 21, 1996. It had 3 sections. The first section merely gave its name: "Defense of Marriage Act". The second section stated that the legality of same sex marriage in one state did not obligate other states to permit it or recognize such a marriage from the other state. The third section defined marriage as the legal union of one man and one woman as husband and wife (and the word spouse referred only to a person of the opposite sex who is a husband or a wife). The Act was challenged repeatedly through the courts. During President Obama's administration, he directed Attorney General Eric Holder to no longer defend DOMA. The House of Representatives took up its defense; however, section 3 was officially ruled unconstitutional by the Supreme Court in the case of Windsor v. Unites States. The entire law would be rendered moot with the Supreme Court's decision in the case of Obergefell v. Hodges that ruled that the fundamental right to marry was guaranteed to same-sex couples. This was found in the 14th Amendment's Equal Protection clause and Due Process clause.

113. A: While choices C, D, and E are all correct to some extent, the best answer involves the lack of coordination among different levels of government. While no individual can truly be prepared for a storm as catastrophic as Katrina, plans for governmental response to such storms are expected to be better organized and executed. President George W. Bush, FEMA director Michael Brown, Louisiana Governor Kathleen Blanco, and New Orleans mayor Ray Nagin were all criticized to some extent over various failures of leadership.

114. D: In March of 1979 a partial meltdown of the reactor core at the 3 Mile Island Nuclear Power plant in Pennsylvania led to a temporary moratorium on licensing new nuclear reactors in the U.S. This significantly slowed the growth of the nuclear power industry in America. The accident was the result of equipment failures combined with human error. The result was a partial release of radioactive gases. The human and environmental impact was very limited; however, the public became more frightened of possible future nuclear disasters. These public fears (based more on ignorance than true knowledge of what happened) lead to the closing of several nuclear power plants. While Nuclear power generation produces no carbon emissions and is thought to be more "green", it is not renewable and therefore not as favored by environmental groups as wind and solar power production. Other Nuclear power plant accidents have had an impact on the public's perception of the safety of nuclear power production, but none as significant for the growth of the industry in the United States as the accident at 3 Mile Island.

115. C: The Peace Corps was part of President Kennedy's "flexible response" to Cold War foreign policy. The Peace Corps had three main goals: promote world peace by helping to meet the needs of interested countries through trained volunteers (teachers, agricultural experts, health care workers, etc.), promote better understanding of Americans by those peoples served, and promote better understanding of other peoples by the American volunteers sent to help. Enthusiastic, idealistic, mainly young Americans volunteered to help third world nations. Part of the hope was to influence third world countries to be pro-western and pro-democracy and keep them from turning to communism.

116. C: During World War II, most of America's manpower was overseas fighting. The women were called to labor in the factories creating equipment and other material for the war. There was a vast need for agricultural laborers. In 1942 America and Mexico entered into an agreement called the Bracero Program. In exchange for tighter border control, America would let Mexican laborers work in the U.S. under short-term contracts. This provided much needed inexpensive labor for farmers along the Mexican/American border needing workers. However, with the lure of employment, many Mexicans came illegally into the U.S. After the war, Farmers on the border had become dependent on cheap seasonal Mexican labor (illegal or legal), so the Bracero program was continued. Others outside of border agriculture started to complain that cheap Mexican labor was keeping blue collar wages artificially low. More and more people wanted the illegal Mexican workers deported. In 1954, President Eisenhower's Attorney General Herbert Brownell, came up with a military style program to round up and deport all illegal Mexican immigrants in the country. The Operation was given a name derived from the practice of Mexican Nationals crossing into the U.S. by swimming the Rio Grande River (Wetback). It is an ethnic slur. The tactics used were sweeping, militaristic, and involved overloading trucks, trains, and ships to try to repatriate Mexican Nationals. In the process many were injured and some died from disease, heat exhaustion, and drowning. Some U.S. citizens were even rounded up and removed in the dragnets used to find illegal immigrants. It is claimed that over 1 million illegal Mexican immigrants were repatriated to Mexico during this operation. That number is disputed as it is almost impossible to determine how many illegal immigrants chose to return home instead of waiting to be deported.

117. B: In December of 1997, in Kyoto, Japan, 41 countries plus the European Union, agreed to cut greenhouse gas emissions to 5.2 percent below 1990 levels. This was done in an effort to reduce certain industrial gas emissions that are believed to create a greenhouse effect in the earth's atmosphere thereby raising the overall global temperature. If true, it could mean the rise of worldwide sea levels, melting of polar ice caps, glaciers, and permafrost on the Tundra. All of which could drastically impact island nations, coastal areas, and flora and fauna worldwide. China, who is currently the world's largest producer of greenhouse gases, was exempted from the protocol because it was deemed a developing nation. The U.S., the second largest producer of greenhouse gases, never formally ratified the protocol. Some nations that did ratify it did not extend it during round two talks in 2012. A new round of talks happened in 2015 in Paris with new provisions.

Some of the provisions of the agreement meant that overall emissions did not have to decrease in a given country as long as they were "offset" by investing in environmentally clean power production and manufacturing in developing countries, or engaging in activities like planting more trees and other things that were seen as helpful to overall climate stability and health.

118. C: During the 1964 U.S. presidential election, incumbent Lyndon Johnson was facing Republican challenger Barry Goldwater. Johnson was leading in all the polls, however his campaign decided to do something that was new. It ran a series of what are known as "attack" ads through 30 to 60 second television commercials. The most famous is known as the Daisy ad (also as the Daisy Girl or Peace, Little Girl). In the commercial a 3 year old girl is seen pulling the petals off of a daisy flower and counting them. She pauses as she reaches 9 and then we hear a countdown of a male voice starting at 10 and counting down to 1. As the announcer counts down the picture of the little girl freezes and then zooms in on her right eye. As the dark pupil of her eye fills the screen the announcer reaches zero and then a huge nuclear explosion is seen, followed by a mushroom cloud. President Johnson is heard in the background saying: "These are the stakes. To make a world in which all of God's children can live, or to go into the dark. We must either love each other, or we must die." Goldwater's name is never mentioned, but the implication was clear. If Goldwater was elected, it would lead the country into a nuclear war with Russia and children would die. Goldwater was known to be very anticommunist and had made statements to the effect that a nuclear war with Russia was winnable. Johnson's campaign wanted to paint Goldwater as an extremist and unstable. The message was plain; a vote for Goldwater was a vote for the destruction of our children.

119. A: In the 1960s U.S. oil production and exploration were starting to decrease. This was not seen as a concern as America merely increased its oil imports from Arab countries. It was believed at the time that the Arab oil exporting countries could not financially afford to decrease their exports to the U.S. Therefore, America felt confident in supporting Israel during the Yom-Kippur war. On Yom-Kippur (an Israeli Jewish holiday) Syria and Egypt along with token forces from Jordan and elsewhere in the Middle East launched an attack against Israel. Russia provided backing and support for the Arabs during the attack, while American provided support for Israel. Israel was victorious in the war. The Organization of Arab Petroleum Exporting Countries (OAPEC) decided to place an embargo on oil exports to the U.S. as retaliation for American's support of Israel. The price of oil skyrocketed which more than made up for the diminished exports to its largest customer, the U.S. The economy of American and other western nations were particularly hard hit. However, most of the damage came from perceived rather than real harm from the embargo. People overreacted and made it worse than it actually was. Growth in the U.S. economy became stagnant while prices rose from the embargo resulting in what was called stagflation. It would take until the 1980s to turn things around from the energy crises of the 1970s.

120. C: On September 11, 2001, Al-Qaeda sponsored terrorists hijacked 4 airplanes. Two of them were flown into the twin towers of the World Trade Center in New York City. One was flown into the Pentagon building in Washington, D.C. The final plane crashed in rural Pennsylvania as the passengers overwhelmed the hijackers, keeping them from striking their intended target. Its intended target was the Capitol Building in Washington, D.C. As a response to these terrorist attacks, President George W. Bush gave a speech to Congress calling for a war on terror. Its primary targets being the overthrow of the Taliban in Afghanistan and Saddam Hussein in Iraq. It was believed that these two countries had helped provide training and support for Al-Qaeda terrorist cells. President Bush also stated that the war on terror would spread anywhere in the world where global terrorism would seek a safe haven. The war in Afghanistan was called Operation Enduring Freedom and the war in Iraq was called Operation Iraqi Freedom. The Taliban government in

Afghanistan was toppled, but there are still Taliban elements are work as well as terrorist groups in Afghanistan. Saddam Hussein's regime was toppled in Iraq and he was executed by the new Iraqi government. However, Iraq has been torn by civil war since Saddam's demise. The war on terror continues.

How to Overcome Test Anxiety

Just the thought of taking a test is enough to make most people a little nervous. A test is an important event that can have a long-term impact on your future, so it's important to take it seriously and it's natural to feel anxious about performing well. But just because anxiety is normal, that doesn't mean that it's helpful in test taking, or that you should simply accept it as part of your life. Anxiety can have a variety of effects. These effects can be mild, like making you feel slightly nervous, or severe, like blocking your ability to focus or remember even a simple detail.

If you experience test anxiety—whether severe or mild—it's important to know how to beat it. To discover this, first you need to understand what causes test anxiety.

Causes of Test Anxiety

While we often think of anxiety as an uncontrollable emotional state, it can actually be caused by simple, practical things. One of the most common causes of test anxiety is that a person does not feel adequately prepared for their test. This feeling can be the result of many different issues such as poor study habits or lack of organization, but the most common culprit is time management. Starting to study too late, failing to organize your study time to cover all of the material, or being distracted while you study will mean that you're not well prepared for the test. This may lead to cramming the night before, which will cause you to be physically and mentally exhausted for the test. Poor time management also contributes to feelings of stress, fear, and hopelessness as you realize you are not well prepared but don't know what to do about it.

Other times, test anxiety is not related to your preparation for the test but comes from unresolved fear. This may be a past failure on a test, or poor performance on tests in general. It may come from comparing yourself to others who seem to be performing better or from the stress of living up to expectations. Anxiety may be driven by fears of the future—how failure on this test would affect your educational and career goals. These fears are often completely irrational, but they can still negatively impact your test performance.

Elements of Test Anxiety

As mentioned earlier, test anxiety is considered to be an emotional state, but it has physical and mental components as well. Sometimes you may not even realize that you are suffering from test anxiety until you notice the physical symptoms. These can include trembling hands, rapid heartbeat, sweating, nausea, and tense muscles. Extreme anxiety may lead to fainting or vomiting. Obviously, any of these symptoms can have a negative impact on testing. It is important to recognize them as soon as they begin to occur so that you can address the problem before it damages your performance.

The mental components of test anxiety include trouble focusing and inability to remember learned information. During a test, your mind is on high alert, which can help you recall information and stay focused for an extended period of time. However, anxiety interferes with your mind's natural processes, causing you to blank out, even on the questions you know well. The strain of testing during anxiety makes it difficult to stay focused, especially on a test that may take several hours. Extreme anxiety can take a huge mental toll, making it difficult not only to recall test information but even to understand the test questions or pull your thoughts together.

Effects of Test Anxiety

Test anxiety is like a disease—if left untreated, it will get progressively worse. Anxiety leads to poor performance, and this reinforces the feelings of fear and failure, which in turn lead to poor performances on subsequent tests. It can grow from a mild nervousness to a crippling condition. If allowed to progress, test anxiety can have a big impact on your schooling, and consequently on your future.

Test anxiety can spread to other parts of your life. Anxiety on tests can become anxiety in any stressful situation, and blanking on a test can turn into panicking in a job situation. But fortunately, you don't have to let anxiety rule your testing and determine your grades. There are a number of relatively simple steps you can take to move past anxiety and function normally on a test and in the rest of life.

Physical Steps for Beating Test Anxiety

While test anxiety is a serious problem, the good news is that it can be overcome. It doesn't have to control your ability to think and remember information. While it may take time, you can begin taking steps today to beat anxiety.

Just as your first hint that you may be struggling with anxiety comes from the physical symptoms, the first step to treating it is also physical. Rest is crucial for having a clear, strong mind. If you are tired, it is much easier to give in to anxiety. But if you establish good sleep habits, your body and mind will be ready to perform optimally, without the strain of exhaustion. Additionally, sleeping well helps you to retain information better, so you're more likely to recall the answers when you see the test questions.

Getting good sleep means more than going to bed on time. It's important to allow your brain time to relax. Take study breaks from time to time so it doesn't get overworked, and don't study right before bed. Take time to rest your mind before trying to rest your body, or you may find it difficult to fall asleep.

Along with sleep, other aspects of physical health are important in preparing for a test. Good nutrition is vital for good brain function. Sugary foods and drinks may give a burst of energy but this burst is followed by a crash, both physically and emotionally. Instead, fuel your body with protein and vitamin-rich foods.

Also, drink plenty of water. Dehydration can lead to headaches and exhaustion, especially if your brain is already under stress from the rigors of the test. Particularly if your test is a long one, drink water during the breaks. And if possible, take an energy-boosting snack to eat between sections.

Along with sleep and diet, a third important part of physical health is exercise. Maintaining a steady workout schedule is helpful, but even taking 5-minute study breaks to walk can help get your blood pumping faster and clear your head. Exercise also releases endorphins, which contribute to a positive feeling and can help combat test anxiety.

When you nurture your physical health, you are also contributing to your mental health. If your body is healthy, your mind is much more likely to be healthy as well. So take time to rest, nourish your body with healthy food and water, and get moving as much as possible. Taking these physical steps will make you stronger and more able to take the mental steps necessary to overcome test anxiety.

Mental Steps for Beating Test Anxiety

Working on the mental side of test anxiety can be more challenging, but as with the physical side, there are clear steps you can take to overcome it. As mentioned earlier, test anxiety often stems from lack of preparation, so the obvious solution is to prepare for the test. Effective studying may be the most important weapon you have for beating test anxiety, but you can and should employ several other mental tools to combat fear.

First, boost your confidence by reminding yourself of past success—tests or projects that you aced. If you're putting as much effort into preparing for this test as you did for those, there's no reason you should expect to fail here. Work hard to prepare; then trust your preparation.

Second, surround yourself with encouraging people. It can be helpful to find a study group, but be sure that the people you're around will encourage a positive attitude. If you spend time with others who are anxious or cynical, this will only contribute to your own anxiety. Look for others who are motivated to study hard from a desire to succeed, not from a fear of failure.

Third, reward yourself. A test is physically and mentally tiring, even without anxiety, and it can be helpful to have something to look forward to. Plan an activity following the test, regardless of the outcome, such as going to a movie or getting ice cream.

When you are taking the test, if you find yourself beginning to feel anxious, remind yourself that you know the material. Visualize successfully completing the test. Then take a few deep, relaxing breaths and return to it. Work through the questions carefully but with confidence, knowing that you are capable of succeeding.

Developing a healthy mental approach to test taking will also aid in other areas of life. Test anxiety affects more than just the actual test—it can be damaging to your mental health and even contribute to depression. It's important to beat test anxiety before it becomes a problem for more than testing.

Study Strategy

Being prepared for the test is necessary to combat anxiety, but what does being prepared look like? You may study for hours on end and still not feel prepared. What you need is a strategy for test prep. The next few pages outline our recommended steps to help you plan out and conquer the challenge of preparation.

Step 1: Scope Out the Test

Learn everything you can about the format (multiple choice, essay, etc.) and what will be on the test. Gather any study materials, course outlines, or sample exams that may be available. Not only will this help you to prepare, but knowing what to expect can help to alleviate test anxiety.

Step 2: Map Out the Material

Look through the textbook or study guide and make note of how many chapters or sections it has. Then divide these over the time you have. For example, if a book has 15 chapters and you have five days to study, you need to cover three chapters each day. Even better, if you have the time, leave an extra day at the end for overall review after you have gone through the material in depth.

If time is limited, you may need to prioritize the material. Look through it and make note of which sections you think you already have a good grasp on, and which need review. While you are studying, skim quickly through the familiar sections and take more time on the challenging parts.

Write out your plan so you don't get lost as you go. Having a written plan also helps you feel more in control of the study, so anxiety is less likely to arise from feeling overwhelmed at the amount to cover.

Step 3: Gather Your Tools

Decide what study method works best for you. Do you prefer to highlight in the book as you study and then go back over the highlighted portions? Or do you type out notes of the important information? Or is it helpful to make flashcards that you can carry with you? Assemble the pens, index cards, highlighters, post-it notes, and any other materials you may need so you won't be distracted by getting up to find things while you study.

If you're having a hard time retaining the information or organizing your notes, experiment with different methods. For example, try color-coding by subject with colored pens, highlighters, or post-it notes. If you learn better by hearing, try recording yourself reading your notes so you can listen while in the car, working out, or simply sitting at your desk. Ask a friend to quiz you from your flashcards, or try teaching someone the material to solidify it in your mind.

Step 4: Create Your Environment

It's important to avoid distractions while you study. This includes both the obvious distractions like visitors and the subtle distractions like an uncomfortable chair (or a too-comfortable couch that makes you want to fall asleep). Set up the best study environment possible: good lighting and a comfortable work area. If background music helps you focus, you may want to turn it on, but otherwise keep the room quiet. If you are using a computer to take notes, be sure you don't have any other windows open, especially applications like social media, games, or anything else that could distract you. Silence your phone and turn off notifications. Be sure to keep water close by so you stay hydrated while you study (but avoid unhealthy drinks and snacks).

Also, take into account the best time of day to study. Are you freshest first thing in the morning? Try to set aside some time then to work through the material. Is your mind clearer in the afternoon or evening? Schedule your study session then. Another method is to study at the same time of day that you will take the test, so that your brain gets used to working on the material at that time and will be ready to focus at test time.

Step 5: Study!

Once you have done all the study preparation, it's time to settle into the actual studying. Sit down, take a few moments to settle your mind so you can focus, and begin to follow your study plan. Don't give in to distractions or let yourself procrastinate. This is your time to prepare so you'll be ready to fearlessly approach the test. Make the most of the time and stay focused.

Of course, you don't want to burn out. If you study too long you may find that you're not retaining the information very well. Take regular study breaks. For example, taking five minutes out of every hour to walk briskly, breathing deeply and swinging your arms, can help your mind stay fresh.

As you get to the end of each chapter or section, it's a good idea to do a quick review. Remind yourself of what you learned and work on any difficult parts. When you feel that you've mastered the material, move on to the next part. At the end of your study session, briefly skim through your notes again.

But while review is helpful, cramming last minute is NOT. If at all possible, work ahead so that you won't need to fit all your study into the last day. Cramming overloads your brain with more information than it can process and retain, and your tired mind may struggle to recall even previously learned information when it is overwhelmed with last-minute study. Also, the urgent nature of cramming and the stress placed on your brain contribute to anxiety. You'll be more likely to go to the test feeling unprepared and having trouble thinking clearly.

So don't cram, and don't stay up late before the test, even just to review your notes at a leisurely pace. Your brain needs rest more than it needs to go over the information again. In fact, plan to finish your studies by noon or early afternoon the day before the test. Give your brain the rest of the day to relax or focus on other things, and get a good night's sleep. Then you will be fresh for the test and better able to recall what you've studied.

Step 6: Take a Practice Test

Many courses offer sample tests, either online or in the study materials. This is an excellent resource to check whether you have mastered the material, as well as to prepare for the test format and environment.

Check the test format ahead of time: the number of questions, the type (multiple choice, free response, etc.), and the time limit. Then create a plan for working through them. For example, if you have 30 minutes to take a 60-question test, your limit is 30 seconds per question. Spend less time on the questions you know well so that you can take more time on the difficult ones.

If you have time to take several practice tests, take the first one open book, with no time limit. Work through the questions at your own pace and make sure you fully understand them. Gradually work up to taking a test under test conditions: sit at a desk with all study materials put away and set a timer. Pace yourself to make sure you finish the test with time to spare and go back to check your answers if you have time.

After each test, check your answers. On the questions you missed, be sure you understand why you missed them. Did you misread the question (tests can use tricky wording)? Did you forget the information? Or was it something you hadn't learned? Go back and study any shaky areas that the practice tests reveal.

Taking these tests not only helps with your grade, but also aids in combating test anxiety. If you're already used to the test conditions, you're less likely to worry about it, and working through tests until you're scoring well gives you a confidence boost. Go through the practice tests until you feel comfortable, and then you can go into the test knowing that you're ready for it.

Test Tips

On test day, you should be confident, knowing that you've prepared well and are ready to answer the questions. But aside from preparation, there are several test day strategies you can employ to maximize your performance.

First, as stated before, get a good night's sleep the night before the test (and for several nights before that, if possible). Go into the test with a fresh, alert mind rather than staying up late to study.

Try not to change too much about your normal routine on the day of the test. It's important to eat a nutritious breakfast, but if you normally don't eat breakfast at all, consider eating just a protein bar. If you're a coffee drinker, go ahead and have your normal coffee. Just make sure you time it so that the caffeine doesn't wear off right in the middle of your test. Avoid sugary beverages, and drink enough water to stay hydrated but not so much that you need a restroom break 10 minutes into the test. If your test isn't first thing in the morning, consider going for a walk or doing a light workout before the test to get your blood flowing.

Allow yourself enough time to get ready, and leave for the test with plenty of time to spare so you won't have the anxiety of scrambling to arrive in time. Another reason to be early is to select a good seat. It's helpful to sit away from doors and windows, which can be distracting. Find a good seat, get out your supplies, and settle your mind before the test begins.

When the test begins, start by going over the instructions carefully, even if you already know what to expect. Make sure you avoid any careless mistakes by following the directions.

Then begin working through the questions, pacing yourself as you've practiced. If you're not sure on an answer, don't spend too much time on it, and don't let it shake your confidence. Either skip it and come back later, or eliminate as many wrong answers as possible and guess among the remaining ones. Don't dwell on these questions as you continue—put them out of your mind and focus on what lies ahead.

Be sure to read all of the answer choices, even if you're sure the first one is the right answer. Sometimes you'll find a better one if you keep reading. But don't second-guess yourself if you do immediately know the answer. Your gut instinct is usually right. Don't let test anxiety rob you of the information you know.

If you have time at the end of the test (and if the test format allows), go back and review your answers. Be cautious about changing any, since your first instinct tends to be correct, but make sure you didn't misread any of the questions or accidentally mark the wrong answer choice. Look over any you skipped and make an educated guess.

At the end, leave the test feeling confident. You've done your best, so don't waste time worrying about your performance or wishing you could change anything. Instead, celebrate the successful completion of this test. And finally, use this test to learn how to deal with anxiety even better next time.

Review Video: Test Anxiety
Visit mometrix.com/academy and enter code: 100340

Important Qualification

Not all anxiety is created equal. If your test anxiety is causing major issues in your life beyond the classroom or testing center, or if you are experiencing troubling physical symptoms related to your anxiety, it may be a sign of a serious physiological or psychological condition. If this sounds like your situation, we strongly encourage you to seek professional help.

Online Resources

Due to our efforts to try to keep this book to a manageable length, we've created a link that will give you access to all of your online resources:

mometrix.com/resources719/clepushistii

It's Your Moment, Let's Celebrate It!

Share your story @mometrixtestpreparation